Day Trips with a Splash

Northeastern Swimming Holes

by Pancho Doll

Running Water Publications
San Diego, California

Read This

Hiking is a potentially dangerous activity. Some sites in this book are reached via unmaintained trails or by overland travel where no trail may be present. As such, they require skill and strength beyond normal requirements for safe hiking. Although the book tries to point out potential dangers, conditions may change on the trail as well as in the water. River levels fluctuate widely during the year. Seasonal indicators are meant as guidelines, not as guarantees of when a place may be safe for swimming. People regularly drown or are seriously injured because they overestimate their abilities or exercise otherwise poor judgement. Rocks in rivers may be steep and slippery. Be cautious and aware even when walking casually in a river or creek bed. Jumping into water from rocks is inherently dangerous. You are responsible for locating submerged obstacles that could cause injury.

The overwhelming majority of swimming holes featured here are entirely on public land. A few cross, or lie near private land that, when visited for this book, did not appear to be posted or were marked with signs giving the public limited permission to use the property. In all events, you must obey no trespassing signs.

Library of Congress Cataloguing-in-Publication Data
Doll, Pancho
Day Trips with a Splash: Northeastern Swimming Holes
Includes Index.
1. Hiking—Northeast—Guide-books.
2. Trails—Northeast—Guide-books.
ISBN 0-9657686-1-9

Acknowledgements

Thanks to my many friends, first among them Tom Coleman in Ludlow, VT for providing the New England research base. Thanks also to Denise Levesque formerly of Conway, NH and to April and Azur Moulaert in Burlington.

Gene Kistler from Blue Ridge Outdoors in Fayetteville, WV provided local wisdom. Cyndi Murry at Mountain State Outfitters in Charleston, WV was also indispensable. Thanks to John Markwell for the variety show he hosts most evenings on the front porch of The Gendarme, his climbing shop at Seneca Rocks, WV.

I'd like to recognize Rick Bayes at the Cathedral Cafe in Fayetteville for fried potatoes and advice on the New River and the Gauley River. My gratitude to Mandy Reiner in Beckley, WV for hot water and alternating current. I extend a trembling, over-caffeinated hand of thanks to Hayden Woodard for free coffee refills when my computer crashed in Charlottesville, VA.

Thank you to Sarah Fellows for supplementary photos and copy editing. Thanks for principal editing to new mother Jill Mahanna, who promised no diaper contents were transferred to my proofs, saying, "even though you handed me a load of crap, I won't return it that way."

The Running Water Staff

Photographer	Duncan Freely
Diving Consultant	Flip Obermore
Spiritual Advisor	Rev. Bob Tism
Wardrobe	Ngo Tan Ligne
Hydrologist	Flo Engover
Topographic Specialist	Hy Cuphill

To my mom for being ever willing to load us kids in the car and take us to the river.

You could tell by the dent of the heel and the sole
They was lots o' fun on hand at the old swimmin' hole

— James Whitcomb Riley (1849-1916)

Maine

New Hampshire & the White Mountains

Vermont & the Green Mountains

Adirondack High Peaks

Susquehanna Headwaters

Monongahela Headwaters

The Gauley, Cranberry & Williams River

Blue Ridge Highlands & New River Gorge

Greenbrier River

Potomac Highlands & Shenandoah Park

Sisyphus Wrecks

A note to young writers; do your book's intro first off. You'll capture the enthusiasm, the aspiration. Wait, and the chances increase that this most important part of your labor will list the misfortunes that can happen during so large a project. Once I lost six months of research in a vehicle burglary. Earlier, I lost an entire vehicle to theft.

If I followed my own advice, I would not be sneaking into the neighbor's yard at night to strip flowers off his dogwood tree. I would not be harassing migratory birds. And I would not be trying to avoid another wry composition on the bitter list of happenstance.

Instead, I installed a big damn lock on the research vessel and traveled cross continent to spend several months wandering the mountains between 70 and 80 degrees west longitude.

Locating swimming holes in eastern states differed from the sparsely populated west. In Virginia the B&B method worked best. Stop at a barbecue place and ask about swimming holes, then follow general directions until you start seeing beer cans. Vermont was simpler: look for naked people.

In the west there was always a dirt road to stop for a tailgate lunch or some sleep. The east has parking lots. Absent a hangtag that says "Outdoor Writer. Do Not Disturb" I had to develop passive means to keep security guards and deputies at arm's length. Opera worked best.

Forget badges and mirrored sunglasses, nothing intimidates like culture. Rossini lets you nap in the handicap space. Blast Wagner and you could do bong hits in front of the courthouse. (That's not direct experience, that last bit.) Rather, I used music to remain unmolested for the hours spent hunched in the research vessel studying topographic lines, looking for what geologists call stratigraphic peculiarities.

Additional peculiarities emerged. They are among the place names listed in the United States Geological Survey. Spend enough time staring at maps and some patterns emerge.

Fewer than 100 miles of Pennsylvania geography separate Hanky Panky Road from Lackawanna County.

Picken's Nose in North Carolina is unlike Booger Hole in West Virginia. It's more like Drip Nose Mountain in Tennessee.

Even if you stand on Dick's Knob in Georgia, you can't see Maude's Crack in Tennessee.

Other than being in Virginia, there appears little similarity between Brushy Butt and Colon Hollow, although I didn't examine either too closely.

It's a rich catalog of names, but one that lacks key elements. Often, swimming holes don't have a commonly recognized name. For many, the book uses the creek or river for the title. When there was more than one spot on the same creek, I sometimes coined names myself.

If place names characterize geography, road signs speak to the times. After the September 2001 attacks, many businesses used their signspace to demonstrate sympathy, a noble sentiment if it stopped there. But they couldn't resist including a commercial message, sometimes with unintended irony.

| New Menu | OR | Super Size Just 39¢ |
| Heaven Help Us | | God Bless America |

All of it would have made a fun summary for 24,000 miles traveling the eastern states, if only I had written it first.

The big damn lock prevented another theft, but a normally dependable disc utility achieved the same result by overwriting five gigabytes of data in one great digital whoosh. The backup had its own problems and after recovery, it was clear that a substantial part of the writing had been chewed into a sticky, wet wad. I felt like that Greek king, the one doomed for eternity to roll a stone up a hill, only to have it break free at the top and tumble back down.

It happened just as the snow was melting. To make deadline I'd have to do two things, write like hell and postpone the approach of summer. I tried to inhibit the northern hemisphere's tilt toward the sun by eliminating the evidence of spring. I'm soaking the yard with herbicide, plucking flowers down to the stem and I'm fighting to keep migratory birds below 40 degrees north latitude.

A book deserves a decent introduction and I wish I had the time to compose one, but right now I have a clear shot at a robin. And I have to take it.

Using this guide

Day Trips with a Splash looks for remote swimming holes. No swimming holes under highway bridges, nothing at boat ramps, major rivers or anyplace so obvious that you wouldn't need a guide book to find it.

The places included are higher in the watershed, above agriculture and municipal runoff. Nearly all are in moving water with solid bedrock surroundings and, where possible, removed from heavy use.

I tried to include a range of difficulties in each chapter, some accessible enough to take small children, others remote and with a high expectation of privacy. But first, a few terms need to be outlined in a quick and dirty glossary so you know what you're getting into.

Moderate scrambling means you might bash a knee or skin an elbow and your friends may laugh at you.

Third-class scrambling means that if you fall, it will hurt. You may receive injuries and your friends might have to help you back to the car. You may even need medical help.

Bushwhacking is considered light if you can do it in shorts. It's moderate if you wish you had pants on. It's heavy if you wish you had pants and boots.

Basins are broad and shallow, usually less than four feet deep. Little or no sense of enclosure.

Pools are deeper, between six and eight feet deep with proportionately less surface area than basins.

Tubs have an even smaller surface area, usually room for only a couple of people. They're five to seven feet deep with near complete enclosure and are most often associated with waterfalls.

Holes are generally the same proportion as a pool but deeper and with a tighter enclosure. If you can dive into it, it's a hole.

CFS means cubic feet per second. It's a measure of water volume.

The Approach

The right-most icon tells how long or difficult the hike is. Most people are familiar with the symbols ski areas use to evaluate the difficulty of the slopes. Here they are redefined for hiking.

 Beginner Less than one-half hour. No more than a couple of tricky steps. You can bring kids.

 Intermediate Up to one hour. May include moderate scrambling, boulder hopping, bushwhacking or amphibious hiking. You feel like a kid.

 Advanced Longer and/or steeper approach. May include extensive boulder hopping, deep river fords or 3rd class scrambling with potentially injurious fall. Leave the kids at home.

 Expert Three-hour approaches over difficult terrain or technical approaches requiring rope. No kidding around.

Some sites in this book are reached via unmaintained trails or by overland travel where no trail may be present. As such, they require skill and strength beyond normal requirements for safe hiking. Although the book tries to point out potential dangers, conditions may change on the trail as well as in the water. You must rely on your own judgement for safety.

HCV means high-clearance vehicle. None of the spots in this book require 4-wheel drive during normal conditions, but many do require a pickup or something other than a passenger car.

US refers to federal highways, primary routes with a typical speed limit of 55 m.p.h.

SR refers to state routes. These are usually two-lane paved roads that lead to most of the destinations in this book.

CR is used for county routes or maintained secondary roads, usually asphalt, but sometimes gravel.

FS is forest service road, often a gravel or even unimproved dirt road.

The Season

The set of icons to the left of the approach icons tell you which season is best for each swimming hole. Remember, conditions vary and there's no reliable way to look at a calendar and judge when a river is safe.

Where available, water gauge information was included in the review. Several places have real-time gauge links on the Internet. Visit www.swimholes.com for those links. Here are some general indicators about season that will be useful in judging water level.

Spring Smaller or dryer watersheds. The spring swimming holes open as soon as the water's warm enough (April or so) and end when the water gets stagnant. The closing varies greatly, but the fourth of July is a good benchmark.

Summer Fourth of July through Labor Day. If the hole has both a spring and a summer designation that means late June through July is best.

Fall As late as October at lower elevations. A summer and a fall combination means water may still be too high in early July and you might have to wait until later in the month.

Entering or crossing water that is moving faster than your ability to navigate it can result in injury. Every year people are injured in moving water that's no more than knee deep.

You can significantly extend your ability using a sturdy aluminum or wooden walking stick. Do not rely on a branch you picked up along the trail. They're never strong enough.

Overall rating

The left-most icon is the overall rating. There are about a dozen points on which to judge the quality of a particular spot. The single most important is water quality. Points are deducted if there's settlement or agricultural runoff upstream, lots of plant glop or brown foam. Beyond water quality, the Holy Trinity of swimming hole quality is height, depth and privacy. Tall, vertical rock gives a sense of enclosure above the waterline and often produces a fat deep end. The ratings are fair, good, excellent and classic.

To get an excellent rating they must have some compelling vertical feature like a fall or a jumping rock. A swimming hole may not be rated classic and also have a boom box designation.

The privacy assessment is based on what you'd expect to find during a peak weekend. Most of the spots are far enough up canyon that if you do meet other people, they're apt to be like-minded outdoors enthusiasts who will enhance the experience rather than detract from it.

> *Doubtful* means one dozen or more people in the area. Bring a bag to pick up trash other people leave behind.

> *Possible* indicates fewer than six people likely. Consider going elsewhere on weekends.

> *Likely* suggests the most you would expect to find is one other group.

> *Guaranteed* says little evidence of visitorship other than a slight trail. If somebody else arrives at the swimming hole, you're probably being followed.

Finding any privacy is difficult in the Northeast. Public land is limited compared to western states. Settlement is more dense and broader. By the time you're in the woods, you're so high in the watershed that the creek barely has enough force to hog out a nice swimming hole. Plus, there are many more people competing for solitude.

The Company

Four icons let you know who or what you can bring for companionship and who you're likely to find.

Kids You're generally safe bringing little dippers of any age to a swimming hole with a beginner's approach. However, short approach holes without a child icon indicates either the rocks are too steep or the water is otherwise inappropriate for junior. On an intermediate approach, a child under seven may tire.

Dogs Many dog owners have difficulty finding places to take their canine pals, what with restrictions on dogs in wilderness areas and national parks. The "Bowser" icon indicates spots in national forests where you don't *have* to keep the dog on a leash and where he's not going to run into lots of other hikers and disturb them. Also where the terrain is appropriate.

The Boom Box Brigades Crowds likely. Potentially rowdy. Likely to be evidence of at least one broken beer bottle.

The Butt indicates one of two things. Either there's a chance you will find skinny dippers (most places in Vermont, for instance) or the place is private enough that you and your companion(s) can opt for no tan lines.

Useability

This is the collection of features that make a swimming hole comfortable for humans. It's difficult to take full enjoyment of a spot if it's too steep to sit down. Bare rock and blazing sun can shorten a day, too.

Seating A well-shaded sand beach is best. Low angle slabs can be very comfortable, especially if the rock has smooth declivities worn in it by the water. These depressions are called *buckets* if they're just big enough for only one to sit in. Seating for two or three is called a *bench seat*. A slab is considered flat if a water bottle rolls slowly enough that you can catch it before it hits the water. It's sloping if you can't set the bottle upright without it tipping over. The slab is considered steep if there's a danger you yourself might tip over. Boulders are less comfortable than slabs. Typically they're more jagged and many are too small to lie on at all. For the purposes of this book, boulders are considered small if they're the size of a trunk. Medium boulders are the size of a car. Large boulders are the size of a cabin and massive boulders are the size of a house.

Sun and shade On what part of the swimming hole will the sun be shining from mid-afternoon on and is there a place you can go to escape it.

Entry and Exit There are more than a few swimming holes you can jump in only to realize there's no easy way back out.

Temperature Water in the mid 60 to 70 degrees is considered just about ideal.

Jumps Basically how high. Where possible I've tried to explain what the bottom features are like. Talk to locals if they're available for safety information, but most importantly get in the water and have a look around for yourself.

You are responsible for your own safety. Anyone jumping from cliffs should not depend solely on this guide for safety information.

Laws

Some jurisdictions prohibit swimming. It's scarcely enforced in most cases and the statutes exists primarily to limit the state's liability. Places where the laws are enforced are noted and listed in the back of the chapter as a means of reminding you not to go there. Whatever the case, you have to obey the directions of the ranger or deputy. Be polite. It is a surprise tactic that will put the ranger off balance and may in the end work to your favor.

The overwhelming majority of swimming holes featured here are entirely on public land. A few cross, or lie near private land that, when visited for this book, did not appear to be posted or were marked with signs giving the public limited permission to use the property. In all events, you must obey no trespassing signs.

The Maps

Material for the 24,000 scale map pages was scanned from United States Geological Survey 7.5-minute topographic maps. In all but a few cases the elevation contours are 40 feet. Every effort was made to get the most current maps; however, trails are often not shown and some other information may be out of date. The 100,000 scale maps were derived from USGS Digital Line Graphs. They are included where driving directions are helpful. Often times, getting to the trailhead is the most difficult part of the trip.

Although it's difficult to get completely lost following a stream or river, it's a good idea to bring a compass on long trips and be proficient in its use.

Where helpful, latitude and longitude annotations were added. Coordinates were checked against digital maps using any one of several commercial mapping software packages. Pinpoint accuracy is what the GPS promises and usually delivers. Still, the possibility for error exists, both in the operation of individual navigation units and in generating coordinates published here. The coordinates and the map location represent a best effort to locate the swimming hole being reviewed, but neither are guaranteed to be accurate beyond 100 meters.

Computer users can get electronic copies of the maps. Send in proof of purchase like the store receipt. Include your web address along with a user name of your choice. Registered users can download the maps to print out at home. Much more elegant than taking the entire book into the hills when you only need two pages.

Finally, it's recommended that you use a forest service recreation map for highway information and for information on campgrounds if you want to make a camping weekend of it.

Tactics and Ethics

The simple fact you're holding this book identifies you as a person of distinction and judgment. You're probably aware of low-impact outdoor ethics, don't cut switchbacks and so forth. Nevertheless, here are a couple things day users should keep in mind.

Don't urinate within 200 feet of open water. For solid waste dig a hole 6 inches deep and in soil exposed to sunlight.

Do not trample grass or vegetation in streambeds. Groups should be fewer than six individuals to avoid unintentional damage.

Don't skid down steep slopes. Rather, place your foot carefully and weight it gingerly so as not to dislodge dirt and rocks. A stealthy tread prevents erosion and avoids twisted ankles. In some cases where there is a steep descent or a stream crossing, it's an excellent idea to bring a ski pole or some sort of sturdy walking stick.

If you want to be a good steward of the outdoors, also bring an empty plastic bag big enough to hold a couple of beer cans or whatever other small bits of trash you may encounter.

Most of the approaches are best done in trail running shoes. Sports sandals are acceptable for the shorter and intermediate ones. Only a few require boots. Remember, he who is shod lightest travels fastest.

Anglers hate it when you jump in a pool that they are fishing. For the most part the prime hours for fishing and those for swimming don't overlap. Fly fishermen typically move up and down the creek. If someone is fly casting a pool, rather than jump in, ask how long they plan to be there and offer to wait until they're finished. If the angler stutters and appears confused, it's because they're not used to swimmers being considerate.

Bait fishermen are a different case. They are apt to stay put for hours, drowning worms while enjoying tobacco products and drinking poor quality beer. About the best tactic is to apologize for the disturbance. Note: It helps if you first exchange some small talk about NASCAR.

The Pro Tour

Everybody wants to discover exciting new places, but anyone who's spent time in the outdoors knows the disappointment of finding trampled flowers in a place that was previously undamaged.

The authors of hiking guides sometimes get the blame.

It is a dilemma. Democratically speaking, everyone has the right to enjoy public land as long as they demonstrate good manners. The problem is we know they don't and that's where egalitarian theory collides with environmentalism.

To refrain from publishing delicate spots isn't the best answer. Outdoor publishers are, after all, in the business of telling readers about cool places to visit. The challenge is how to limit the information about unspoiled venues to people who will use them with care.

Hence, the Pro Tour.

It's a small collection of places that were either too sensitive to absorb general use. Other entries are on private land where there's limited right to pass, but a danger that additional careless users might cause the landowner to close access. It's available to members of outdoor or environmental groups like the Appalachian Mountain Club, Nature Conservancy, Environmental Defense, or any local group that identifies you a good outdoor citizen.

The Pro Tour is available for a small fee. Send a copy of your membership card and a check for $3.95 to the address below.

Running Water Publications
5694 Mission Center Rd. #170
San Diego, Ca. 92108

Baxter Park, Androscoggin Piscataquis, Kennebec, & Saco River Headwaters

Big Niagra Falls

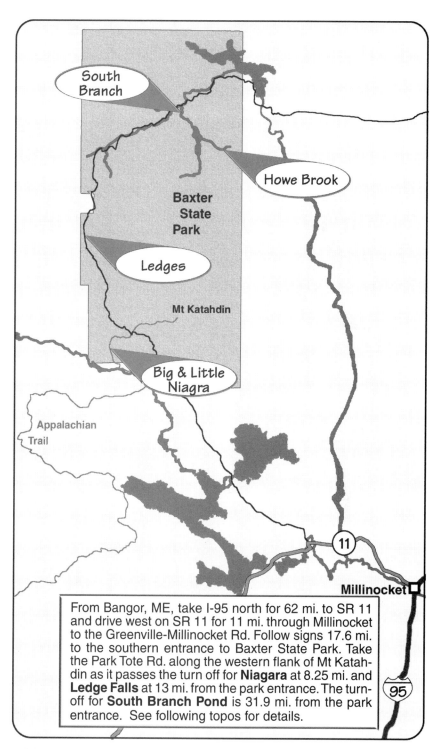

South
Branch

Howe Brook

Baxter
State
Park

Ledges

Mt Katahdin

Big & Little
Niagra

Appalachian
Trail

11

Millinocket

95

From Bangor, ME, take I-95 north for 62 mi. to SR 11 and drive west on SR 11 for 11 mi. through Millinocket to the Greenville-Millinocket Rd. Follow signs 17.6 mi. to the southern entrance to Baxter State Park. Take the Park Tote Rd. along the western flank of Mt Katahdin as it passes the turn off for **Niagara** at 8.25 mi. and **Ledge Falls** at 13 mi. from the park entrance. The turn-off for **South Branch Pond** is 31.9 mi. from the park entrance. See following topos for details.

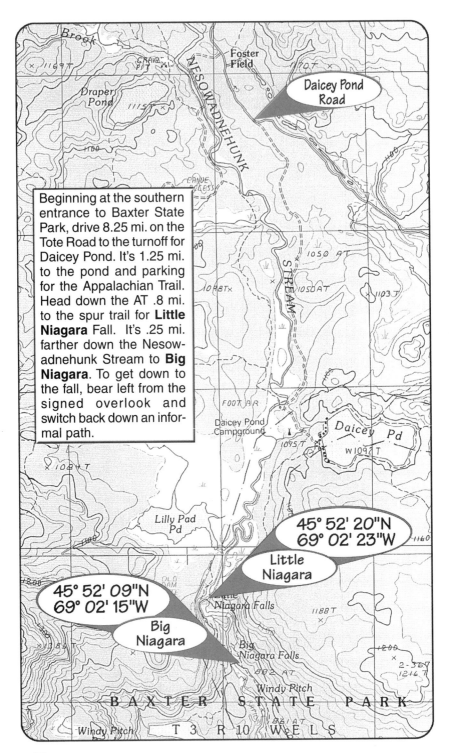

Daicey Pond Road

Beginning at the southern entrance to Baxter State Park, drive 8.25 mi. on the Tote Road to the turnoff for Daicey Pond. It's 1.25 mi. to the pond and parking for the Appalachian Trail. Head down the AT .8 mi. to the spur trail for **Little Niagara** Fall. It's .25 mi. farther down the Nesowadnehunk Stream to **Big Niagara**. To get down to the fall, bear left from the signed overlook and switch back down an informal path.

45° 52' 20"N 69° 02' 23"W

Little Niagara

45° 52' 09"N 69° 02' 15"W

Big Niagara

Niagara Fall

The two most dramatic water features in Baxter State Park. (That's Little Niagara above. Big Niagara is pictured full page at the front of the chapter.) A large granite outcrop with a narrow notch sends Nesowadnehunk Stream tumbling 22 vertical feet into a broad basin. Downstream a log has washed up against a cedar. You sit on it under low, dense conifer shade with 20 feet of sand beach in front of you, while the pink Katahdin granite and the dark green Nesowadnehunk slash across your frame of view. If your tired feet are working their way up the Appalachian Trail, or if you got a book of poetry for your birthday, Little Niagara has what is positively the best place to relax and reflect.

The main show is downstream at Big Niagara. It's a two-tier fall, broad at the top, then compressed to half width at midpoint before the water spills into a very large hole interspersed with islands of water worn, granite blocks. The largest island is high enough that it has trees growing there. At the water level pictured above, it was possible to boulder hop to the island and use it as a base camp for an afternoon of river fun.

The main hole is really spectacular. Sixty to 70 feet long. Water is faster and you have to be paddling if you are in it. Little chance of being pulled downstream and getting smashed, but it's not a lazy bobbing pool. Best seating on the west on almost a half an acre of slabs. In sum, a classic.

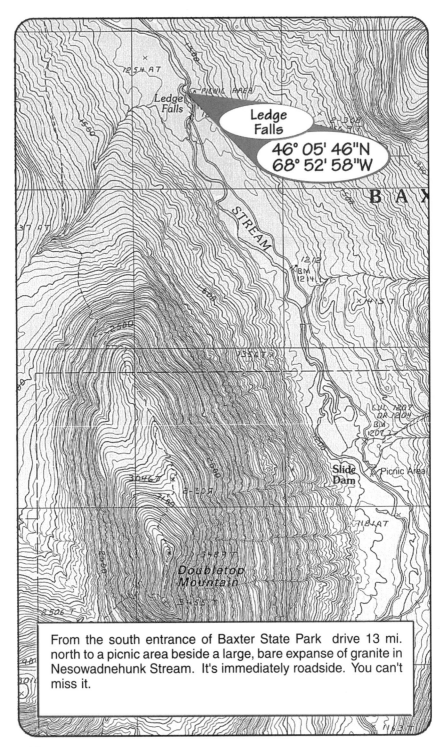

Ledge
Falls

**46° 05' 46"N
68° 52' 58"W**

From the south entrance of Baxter State Park drive 13 mi. north to a picnic area beside a large, bare expanse of granite in Nesowadnehunk Stream. It's immediately roadside. You can't miss it.

Ledge Fall

Baby's first swimming hole. It's the broadest slide I ever saw, right by the road and at a low pitch so you don't have to worry about the little dippers tipping over and washing downstream. It's got a couple of small pools and shallow drops that are on a perfect scale for the little ones. The granite is so well polished by the Nesowadnehunk Stream that any wet surface, though not dangerous, is very slick. I watched a novice fly fisherman do a slow-motion slide into the top pool. Once his boots broke traction, he and about $3,500 dollars of Orvis gear slipped at a rate of one foot per second into the deep end. The entire process took long enough for me to say three times, "I wish I had a video camera."

There are actually several reasons I'd tend not to review this place. It's directly on the road. The "fall" is really just a low cascade, and the pools really aren't deep enough for adults to fully immerse. But there's something compelling about the wide shoulders of granite on both sides of a sun-drenched river.

Recreation in Baxter State Park is heavily managed to reduce impact. You may need reservations simply to get in. The day fee is $8 for out-of-state vehicles. Vehicles with Maine registration enter free of charge. Note that the roads are few and narrow. No vehicles over 22 feet long are permitted.

For reservations phone (207) 723-5140.

Maine

46° 05' 46"N
68° 52' 58"W

Howe Brook

South Branch Pond

46° 07'09"N
68° 54' 55"W

Follow the previous map for Baxter State Park to the turnoff for **South Branch Pond**. Drive 2.1 mi. to parking and walk through the campground to lean-to # 10 and the Pogy Notch Trail. Hike south following blue blazes .75 mi. then left onto the **Howe Brook Trail**. It's .2 mi. to the lowest fall and another quarter mile to the second fall. For **South Branch Pond** begin at the ranger station and paddle .8 mi.(canoe livery available) the length of Lower South Branch Pond. Drag the short distance between the lower and upper pond, then resume paddling another .3 mi. to an obvious rock wall on the west shore of the lake.

South Branch Pond

Reliable sources report that the water is more than 40 feet deep below this tall rock face. I'm not saying that you can huck your carcass 60 feet or so from the top. I'm not even saying you should jump from the intermediate ledges at 10, 15 and 20 feet. All I'm reporting is that were you to attempt any of these things, the reliable source assures that you would not be the first.

This chunk of rock is uncommon in that it seems difficult to find tall rock adjoining deep water in this part of the country. South Branch Pond is even more notable because it's remote compared to, for example, Frye's Leap on Sebago Lake. But it's not an epic trip that'll take all weekend to reach. Great choice if you want to discover a less visited part of Baxter State Park.

Follow directions on the map opposite. Tie your boat to a snag on the southern end of the outcrop right below the lower ledges. The rock is really solid. Not lots of seating because it's all pretty steep. Use caution scrambling above the lower ledges. There are lots of pebbles from the decomposing rock that can be like walking on ball bearings. There are few hand holds, making it difficult to climb back down. Injuries frequently occur this way.

Howe Brook

Howe Brook

Howe Brook has three falls marked on the topographic map for Baxter State Park. The uppermost, while attractive, doesn't pool. The two lower falls are separated by a steep process of cascades and potholes, some of which are themselves worth inspection, if not disrobing.

A few hundred yards from the trail junction (see previous map) is the place to send the kids. It's a small pool with easy entry and exit. It's only hip deep, so of little interest to an adult, but a different matter if you're in fourth grade. Prettiest thing about it is a pair of white pines shading it on the northern bank. Above that is what's by far the deepest hole on the creek. Twins spouts have helped grind out a nice, deep tub. It has plenty of seating up above. A more scenic place, you couldn't hope for. This would be the main destination.

Above, a cascade runs in perfect little rivulets with beautiful symmetry and conformation. Water enters the center of a chin-deep pool with truckloads of baseball and softball-sized rocks. Somebody really needs to get in there with a backhoe. Absolutely beautiful spot regardless.

There is a smaller, tighter fall above. It has a 20-foot cascade. At the north side, (trail side) is a vertical wall, 15 feet high with a basin below that may offer some privacy. Be extremely careful of footing. Any wet rock can send you sailing.

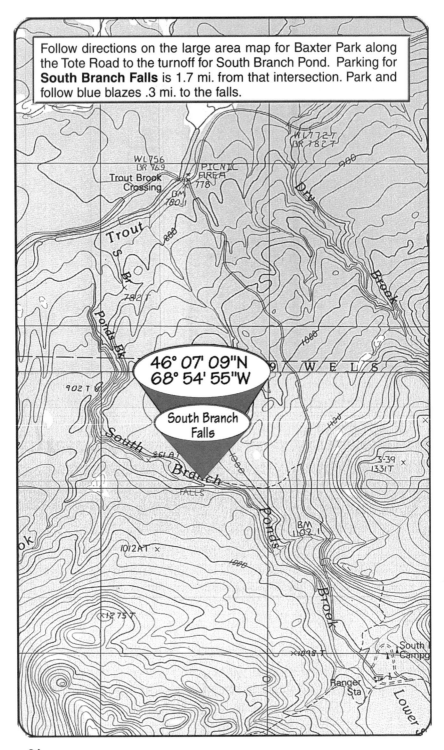

Follow directions on the large area map for Baxter Park along the Tote Road to the turnoff for South Branch Pond. Parking for **South Branch Falls** is 1.7 mi. from that intersection. Park and follow blue blazes .3 mi. to the falls.

46° 07' 09"N
68° 54' 55"W

South Branch
Falls

South Branch Falls

Here is a swimming hole best characterized by joints. A rhyolite crag stands almost 40 feet above South Branch Falls. To reach the pool, walk downstream from the ledge and scramble down to the creek. The hole is very narrow and about 70 feet long. It is apt to be a little warmer than similar streams at this latitude because the water originates from the surface of South Branch Pond where it's been collecting solar energy all day.

On your way to the water you may notice that some of the rock is fractured into generally hexagonal shapes that look like paving stones. They're columnar joints, a manner of fracturing that happens when extrusive rock like this cools slowly. The phenomenon is more evident at low water levels where a longitudinal view shows the length of the columns.

Back at the top of the crag, a ledge serves as an excellent over-view. One misstep, you'd fall and break your neck, it seems. But the ledge slopes away from the water such that you could sit with your feet dangling in the air, and if second hand smoke from the funny cigarettes your friend likes were to make you fall asleep, you would simply flop over backwards. It's a delightful place to visit and far less traveled than any of the other Baxter State Park swimming holes in this book.

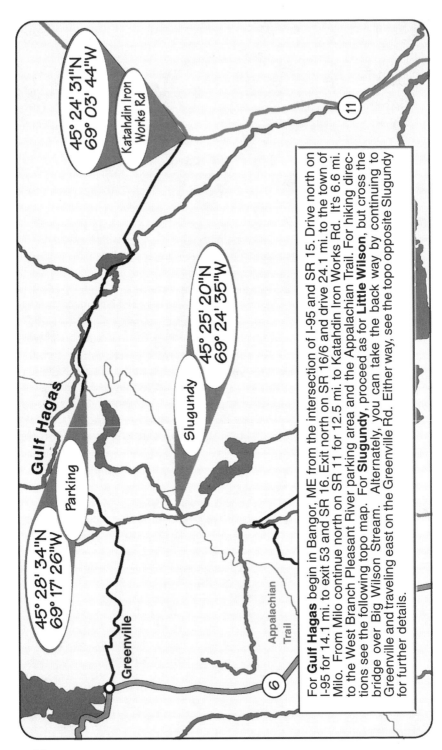

45° 24' 31"N
69° 03' 44"W

Katahdin Iron
Works Rd

11

45° 25' 20"N
69° 24' 35"W

Slugundy

Gulf Hagas

Parking

45° 28' 34"N
69° 17' 26"W

Greenville

6

Appalachian
Trail

For **Gulf Hagas** begin in Bangor, ME from the intersection of I-95 and SR 15. Drive north on I-95 for 14.1 mi. to exit 53 and SR 15. Exit north on SR 16/6 and drive 24.1 mi. to the town of Milo. From Milo continue north on SR 11 for 12.5 mi. to Katahdin Iron Works Rd. It's 6.6 mi. to the West Branch Pleasant River parking area and the Appalachian Trail. For hiking directions see the following topo map. For **Slugundy**, proceed as for **Little Wilson**, but cross the bridge over Big Wilson Stream. Alternately, you can take the back way by continuing to Greenville and traveling east on the Greenville Rd. Either way, see the topo opposite Slugundy for further details.

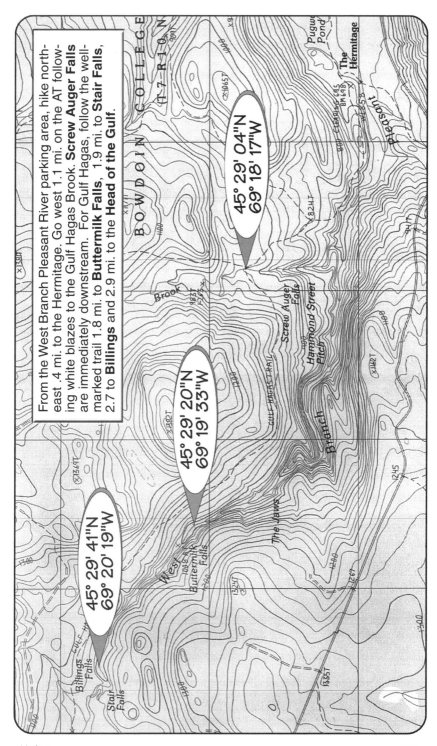

From the West Branch Pleasant River parking area, hike northeast .4 mi. to the Hermitage. Go west 1.1 mi. on the AT following white blazes to the Gulf Hagas Brook. **Screw Auger Falls** are immediately downstream. For Gulf Hagas, follow the well-marked trail 1.8 mi. to **Buttermilk Falls**, 1.9 mi. to **Stair Falls**, 2.7 to **Billings**, 2.9 mi. to the **Head of the Gulf.**

45° 29' 04"N
69° 18' 17"W

45° 29' 20"N
69° 19' 33"W

45° 29' 41"N
69° 20' 19"W

Screwauger Fall

Screwauger Falls

Gulf Hagas Brook creates several mid-sized falls on its way to the West Branch of the Pleasant River. At the upper fall, twin spouts 15 feet tall have bored out a steep, narrow hole about 20 feet across and eight feet long. Features include interesting rock sculpting along with some great ledges for relaxing on the left bank. The water gets out among some scattered boulders with a nice gravel pocket on the right hand side, then runs about 100 feet to a middle fall.

To reach the middle fall you continue beyond the sign that reads "viewpoint." This middle fall is even better than the upper one. It's a plunge into a deep, deep tank about 25 feet long and trapezoidal in shape. Water spills out over huge, huge slabs of rock. There is a blocky wall on the right that rises 35 to 40 feet. A white pine growing right out of one of the rocks makes a beautiful garnish.

Just below that is another fall with two small pools in the shape of an hourglass. The second pool flares at the bottom of vertical, even undercut walls, about 60 to 70 feet wide. These two pools are very deep and tight. Difficult entry and exit make this third fall not too user friendly.

Doesn't seem to be much privacy at Screwauger. Heavy traffic means this place is best visited on weekdays only.

Buttermilk Falls

Gulf Hagas is a steep, often narrow, cut of post-glacial age. It contains five falls and several rapids occurring over a total drop of 400 feet. It's considered one of New England's outstanding scenic areas, the subject of postcards and a destination for several generations of hikers and nature lovers. It carries a high volume of water, arising mostly in commercially owned softwood forests. The water is quite dark in color but has no odor .

Buttermilk is the tallest fall on the gorge at 25 feet. The face is 15 to 20 feet wide and rolls into a bodacious pool that's easily 60 feet wide and 50 feet long. Huge. Wide. Beautiful. Water is likely to be moving, though. You can't just lollygag around. Brisk temperature helps you keep active. Ryan Smith of Rocklin pronounced the chilly temp perfect for a native "Maine-iac."

"It's the best solution for the sticky, hot summer days in Maine." He recommends swimming to a little cove on the far left of Buttermilk Falls, next to an old cedar snag. "Feel your way up to flat outcrop," he said. "The jump is about 10 feet. The water's deep. No worries."

It's a weekday classic. Many, too many, visitors on weekends. A somewhat complicated approach down the steep canyon walls keeps the casual hikers on the rim above Buttermilk. They prefer Stair Falls, just above Buttermilk.

Billings Falls

The West Branch of the Pleasant River is split into two channels by a large island at the head of Gulf Hagas. They converge just above Billings Falls and form a near vertical drop of 12 feet. Viewed from the overlook, the swimming hole below the fall is a steep arc of metamorphic rock around a kidney-shaped pool that is simply immense. From the fall to the outlet the pool measures 90 feet long. It's mondo deep and churning where the fall drops in. Some table-sized flakes are scattered at the bottom; they're good for relaxation.

Getting to water level is a little tricky. Look for a scrambling descent to the right of the overlook, then boulder hop to the pool. For easier, though less dramatic, fun go to the Step Falls at the head of Gulf Hagas. It's less than 200 yards above Billings.

Step Fall is a multichannel cascade. Nothing really deep enough to swim in, but at least 4,000 square feet of sunny rock on which to recline and soak in the season. In addition, it's much less crowded than the lower part of Gulf Hagas. Officials said that one third of the visitors turn around at Screwauger Falls with only 160 people a day making it to Step Falls. It's half that on a weekday. That may be a high estimate since land managers never underestimate the number of visitors.

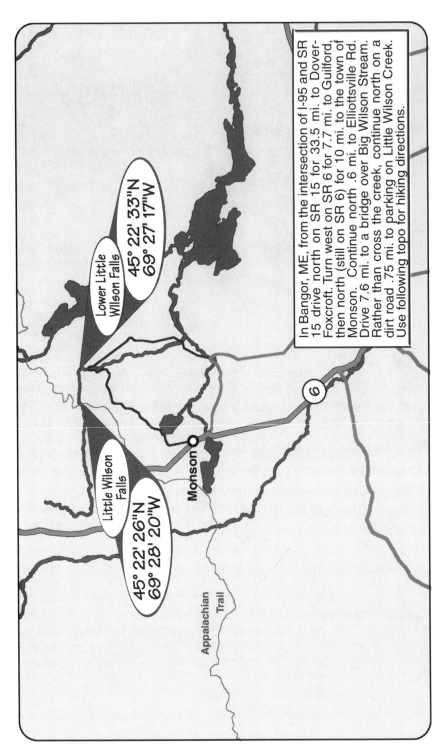

Lower Little Wilson Falls
45° 22' 33"N
69° 27' 17"W

Little Wilson Falls
45° 22' 26"N
69° 28' 20"W

Monson

Appalachian Trail

⑥

In Bangor, ME, from the intersection of I-95 and SR 15 drive north on SR 15 for 33.5 mi. to Dover-Foxcroft. Turn west on SR 6 for 7.7 mi. to Guilford, then north (still on SR 6) for 10 mi. to the town of Monson. Continue north .6 mi. to Elliottsville Rd. Drive 7.6 mi. to a bridge over Big Wilson Stream. Rather than cross the creek, continue north on a dirt road .75 mi. to parking on Little Wilson Creek. Use following topo for hiking directions.

Little Wilson Stream

Several swimming holes, all accessed from a large parking area next to an overused hole. I prefer a place upstream where a tremendous flood from the not-too-distant past chipped out a chunk of rock about the size of a dump truck bed. You can discern where the rock used to be before it was shoved 25 feet up a ramp to where it's perched as level as a table above a pool that's 10 feet by 20 feet.

Flow in this watershed is not always so forceful. Author and paddler Zip Kellog once parked below Greenville intending to paddle one half day to Big Wilson Stream. The trip ended two days later.

"When we got to the start, the water that was coming out of the dam you could have caught in a teacup," he said. "We started anyway, hoping that we'd encounter a downstream tributary that would add enough water to float the boats."

They didn't. After dragging through mud and gravel for hours, they decided to walk out. They returned with friends the next day to drag the craft through the near waterless drainage.

"When we got to where we could float, we all jumped in the canoes. Not long afterward a warden stopped us. The extra people meant we didn't have a flotation device for each person and he cited us."

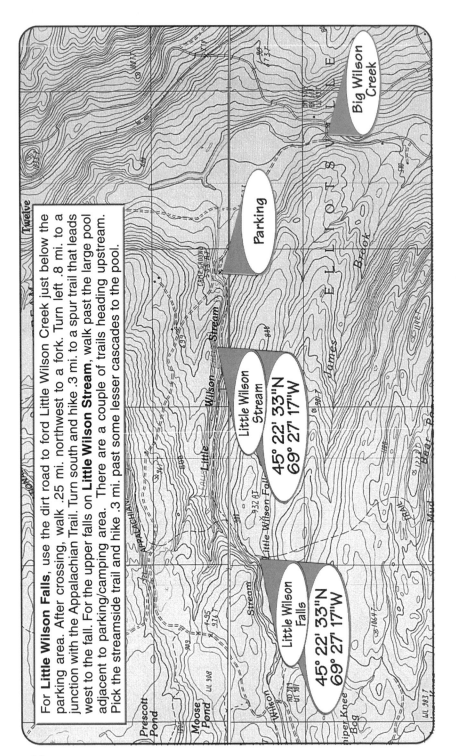

For **Little Wilson Falls**, use the dirt road to ford Little Wilson Creek just below the parking area. After crossing, walk .25 mi. northwest to a fork. Turn left .8 mi. to a junction with the Appalachian Trail. Turn south and hike .3 mi. to a spur trail that leads west to the fall. For the upper falls on **Little Wilson Stream**, walk past the large pool adjacent to parking/camping area. There are a couple of trails heading upstream. Pick the streamside trail and hike .3 mi. past some lesser cascades to the pool.

Big Wilson Creek

Parking

Little Wilson Stream
45° 22' 33"N
69° 27' 17"W

Little Wilson Falls
45° 22' 33"N
69° 27' 17"W

Little Wilson Falls

The principal drop at Little Wilson Falls ranks among the tallest in the state, approximately 40 feet. The pool below is smallish and barely overhead deep. The water has a slightly brown tint, but no odor. What's unusual, what makes the fall so interesting, is the incredibly angular, blocky appearance of the rock. It's slate that's been uplifted so that the cleavages are nearly vertical and the tops of the rock are fractured off very evenly. More than anything it looks like an astrophysical crystal formation with six feet of water in the bottom of it.

The gorge continues a little less than one quarter mile below the fall. At places the walls are close to 100 feet above the stream and nearly vertical. It's mainly a rapid, but there are several additional falls of eight feet or better. Horizontal features are good also. Some natural benches have formed out of lateral cleavage in the slate. It's a small watershed, which is good, given the tight, muscular character of the gorge. I'd estimate that a flow above three cubic feet per second would make it unsafe, or at least uncomfortable, for swimming.

Note: Don't be misled by a smaller fall at the first stream crossing after you turn from the logging road onto the AT . That's just the discharge from Moose Pond. Little Wilson Gorge is farther south on the AT. See the map at left.

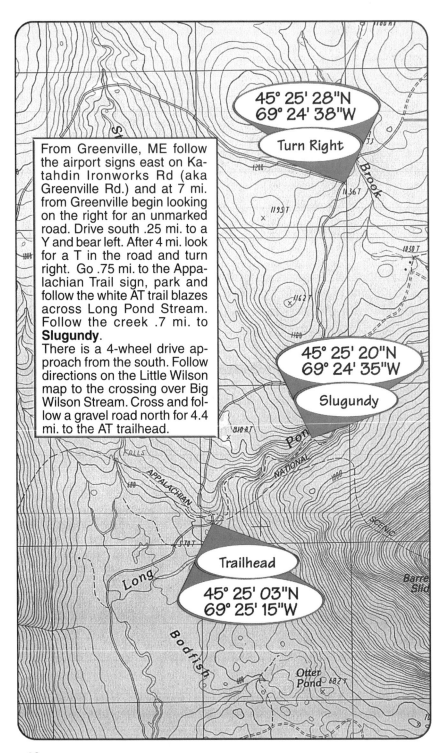

45° 25' 28"N
69° 24' 38"W

Turn Right

From Greenville, ME follow the airport signs east on Katahdin Ironworks Rd (aka Greenville Rd.) and at 7 mi. from Greenville begin looking on the right for an unmarked road. Drive south .25 mi. to a Y and bear left. After 4 mi. look for a T in the road and turn right. Go .75 mi. to the Appalachian Trail sign, park and follow the white AT trail blazes across Long Pond Stream. Follow the creek .7 mi. to **Slugundy**.

There is a 4-wheel drive approach from the south. Follow directions on the Little Wilson map to the crossing over Big Wilson Stream. Cross and follow a gravel road north for 4.4 mi. to the AT trailhead.

45° 25' 20"N
69° 24' 35"W

Slugundy

Trailhead

45° 25' 03"N
69° 25' 15"W

Slugundy

"**Slewgundy**: A site along a stream where the water flows through a tortuous channel which acts as a deterrent to log driving. Sometimes modified to slugundy."

— Maine State Planning Office.

In this case it's a long process of falls and cascades filling a small gorge 800 feet long on a spur to the Appalachian Trail. At the head is a pair of falls just over 10 feet high that occur one after the other. From there the creek bends sharply into a rifle sight trough for 50 fast, churning feet.

The rock is aligned very closely with the water's flow and the creek has chipped out some big pieces, leaving sides that are steep, though not very tall. The pool is created principally by a couple of medium boulders slipped into the bottom of the gorge. They raise the level by 3 to 4 feet. Another well-placed boulder would make a great hole. Walls are usually sheer on only one side, so it fails to create anything more than seven feet deep. The top pool is probably 25 feet long, 10 feet wide and six to seven feet deep at the top where the sweet spot is. It has a nice place to haul out on the northern side, where there are some beautifully smooth ledges streaked with quartz.

I estimate it's best during low water conditions because the channel is so tight — such a slewgundy — that water is to too fast otherwise.

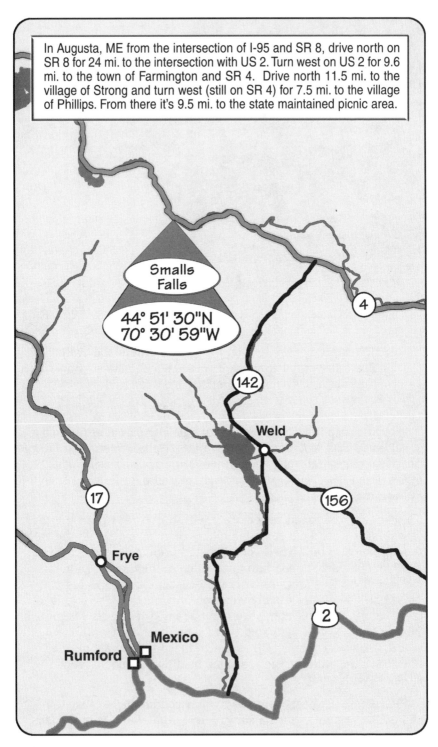

In Augusta, ME from the intersection of I-95 and SR 8, drive north on SR 8 for 24 mi. to the intersection with US 2. Turn west on US 2 for 9.6 mi. to the town of Farmington and SR 4. Drive north 11.5 mi. to the village of Strong and turn west (still on SR 4) for 7.5 mi. to the village of Phillips. From there it's 9.5 mi. to the state maintained picnic area.

Smalls
Falls

44° 51' 30"N
70° 30' 59"W

4

142

Weld

17

156

Frye

2

Mexico

Rumford

Smalls Falls

The Sandy River drops a total of 60 feet in a series of falls and cascades, including four near vertical drops with smooth, round pools of at least 20 feet in diameter. The lowest hole is the largest. It's a funnel shape at least 30 feet long and 20 feet wide. At the top of it is a wedding cake fall that's around 12 feet high and very scenic. It adjoins a state maintained rest area and it's easily accessible. A footbridge crosses the river below the hole and a footpath turns right up the steep canyon.

You pass a couple of holes that are fenced off and too steep to be practical, anyway. (It'd be worth it to rappel down into them if they were remote, wilderness swimming holes, but no need to go through all that just to have a dozen people watching you.) The fourth pool from the bottom is quite dipable. A collar of rock makes a dandy impound and a good deep end. Here near the top of the gorge the contour spaces out some and there's plenty of smooth level rock to relax on.

Back at the bottom of the canyon, you'll find more pools. Instead of turning right at the bridge you can continue straight up a tributary with four to five pools and tubs. The setting is more like a woodland stream, more intimate, less dramatic and less visited. Expectation of privacy is fair on a weekend and there are a couple of places where privacy will be excellent on a weekday.

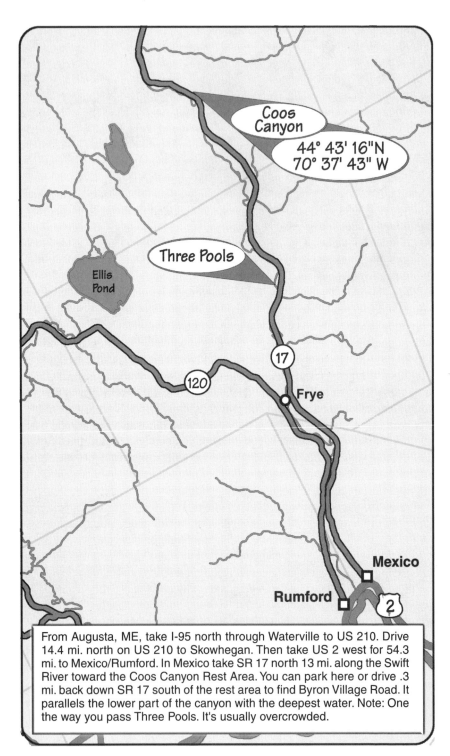

From Augusta, ME, take I-95 north through Waterville to US 210. Drive 14.4 mi. north on US 210 to Skowhegan. Then take US 2 west for 54.3 mi. to Mexico/Rumford. In Mexico take SR 17 north 13 mi. along the Swift River toward the Coos Canyon Rest Area. You can park here or drive .3 mi. back down SR 17 south of the rest area to find Byron Village Road. It parallels the lower part of the canyon with the deepest water. Note: One the way you pass Three Pools. It's usually overcrowded.

Coos Canyon

The bottom drops out of the Swift River producing fabulously deep water running between vertical walls as high as 32 feet. Cory Freeman grew up jumping into the water he estimates is 20 feet deep in places. As a boy he even dreamed of becoming a professional cliff diver before he discovered that the paper mill offered more immediate employment. So he repairs boilers four days a week and spends summer afternoons testing gravity in the canyon. His best safety tip is that most people get injured climbing down from something they are too scared to jump from.

"If you're going to climb up, jump or walk off the top. Don't try to climb back down," he said.

Down climbing is not the *only* way to get hurt. Ryan Plourde, also of Rumford, points to a jagged scar he got from head butting a piece of slate.

"Somebody jumped in at a spot and said that the water was deep enough. It was my turn and everybody was looking at me, so I dived. When I came up I was bleeding. It hurt pretty bad for a while. Now it's just numb."

I asked how deep the numbness went and a friend said, "all the way to the collarbone."

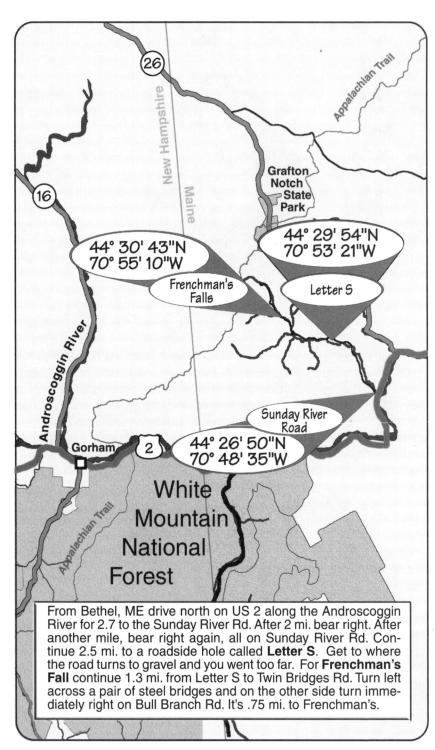

44° 30' 43"N
70° 55' 10"W

Frenchman's
Falls

44° 29' 54"N
70° 53' 21"W

Letter S

Sunday River
Road

44° 26' 50"N
70° 48' 35"W

White
Mountain
National
Forest

Gorham

From Bethel, ME drive north on US 2 along the Androscoggin River for 2.7 to the Sunday River Rd. After 2 mi. bear right. After another mile, bear right again, all on Sunday River Rd. Continue 2.5 mi. to a roadside hole called **Letter S**. Get to where the road turns to gravel and you went too far. For **Frenchman's Fall** continue 1.3 mi. from Letter S to Twin Bridges Rd. Turn left across a pair of steel bridges and on the other side turn immediately right on Bull Branch Rd. It's .75 mi. to Frenchman's.

Step Falls

Frenchman's Falls

A popular place that nobody can find. Frenchman's is tucked up on a tributary to the Sunday River near a local trail leading to the Appalachian Trail. Several times when I told people that I'd be looking for swimming holes in Maine they'd say something like, "Yeah, there's supposed to be someplace called Frenchman's. We looked, but never found it."

It's a small, deep pool fed by a plunge fall seven or eight feet tall. The pool is reputed to be twice as deep and, although I didn't have a plumb line to test the claim, it's certainly deep enough to catch the dozens of kids apt to jump into it on a summer day. Frenchman's happens where a bubble of granite popped up among some less distinguished rock. The granite really lends itself to hydraulic sculpting; in addition, it has excellent traction.

About 30 feet above the fall is a low cascade that stretches the entire 20 foot width of the brook. It's very pretty and the rest of the creek up to the trailhead parking is just as enchanting. It's all clear water from a mountain stream with hardly any muck, yuck or funk. You will encounter some litter along the dirt road where people picnic, but nothing like broken glass or other odious items in the river.

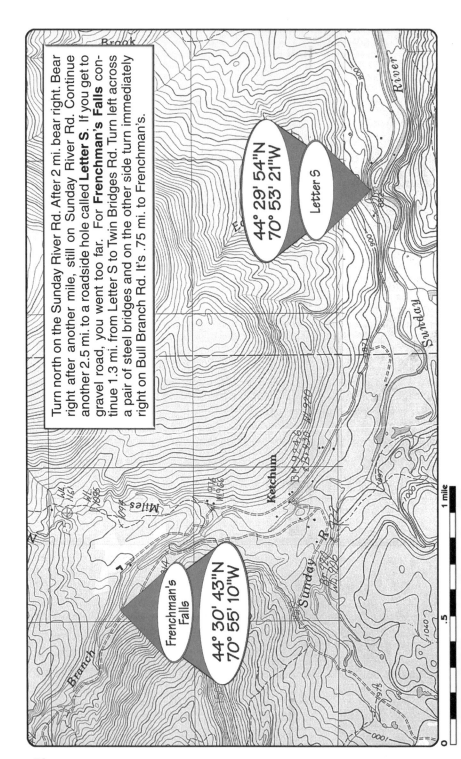

Turn north on the Sunday River Rd. After 2 mi. bear right. Bear right after another mile, still on Sunday River Rd. Continue another 2.5 mi. to a roadside hole called **Letter S**. If you get to gravel road, you went too far. For **Frenchman's Falls** continue 1.3 mi. from Letter S to Twin Bridges Rd. Turn left across a pair of steel bridges and on the other side turn immediately right on Bull Branch Rd. It's .75 mi. to Frenchman's.

44° 29' 54"N
70° 53' 21"W

Letter S

Frenchman's Falls

44° 30' 43"N
70° 55' 10"W

Letter S

The only thing missing is a stripe painted on the bottom. Letter S is so long that it's made for lap swimming. You can start 80 feet below the top of the hole and stroke upstream through the fat part of the pool toward a wide breech in a low, massive rock wall. Water velocity increases the higher you swim into a progressively narrow channel. Depending on the river level you might make it to the top. More likely you'll reach a point of equilibrium and then it's fun to see how long you can maintain position without getting pushed back.

If any of this is too Type A for you, well there's plenty of water to bob around with your beverage of choice. (No glass bottles.) The pool at the bottom is enormous and the water quality is excellent. Just a wee bit of moss was beginning to grow on downstream rocks, and this during extremely low water and record high temperatures. It has a sandy bottom with what must be mica or pyrites that glitter and flash in the sun.

It's off to the side of a dead end road. It runs west to east, which is to say it's very open with lots of sun. The seating is a little limited though. There is room for one group on the near side, but there's more rock on the far side if you can swim across without getting your towel wet.

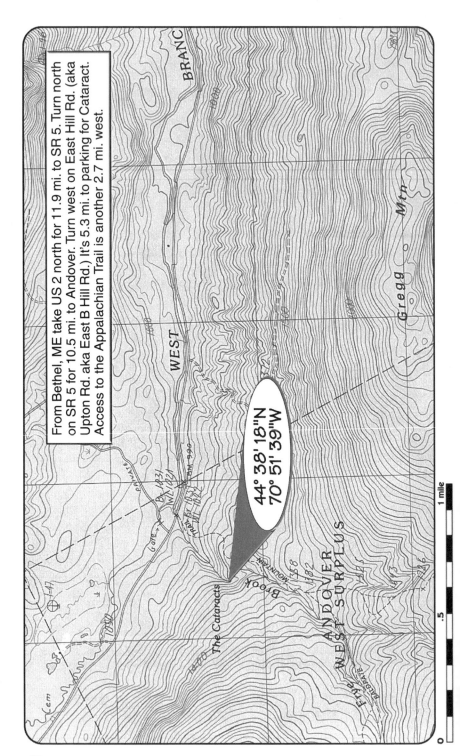

From Bethel, ME take US 2 north for 11.9 mi. to SR 5. Turn north on SR 5 for 10.5 mi. to Andover. Turn west on East Hill Rd. (aka Upton Rd. aka East B Hill Rd.) It's 5.3 mi. to parking for Cataract. Access to the Appalachian Trail is another 2.7 mi. west.

44° 38' 18"N
70° 51' 39"W

Cataracts

Frye Brook takes several leaps during its descent to the West Branch of the Ellis River. There are three falls, with the uppermost being the star. It's a flume perfectly incised into the granite, a single concentrated channel of water that shoots out in an eight-foot plunge. The pool below is small, but exquisite. A beautiful oval is struck into the rock, 10 feet on the major axis and six feet on the minor. Below that is a second fall with a broader pool and much more relaxed angles. It's 20 feet in diameter and six to seven feet deep in the middle. There's one good lounging rock at the top of the pool near the fall.

Follow directions on the topo map at left to reach the trail. Walk south on an abandoned dirt road to a fork. Bear right toward the creek and follow yellow blazes on the Cataract Trail. The trail climbs steeply on the south bank of Frye Brook to a point that it's nearly hand over hand for a short distance. Once at the top, cross the creek well above the fall. Once on the far side, stay up in the trees above the water. Circle around toward the fall and make a couple of long down steps to a crack directly above a fixed rope. It's much safer than going direct.

Liabilities are that it points due north. Taken together with the heavy canopy means little sunlight. Consequently, the rock has lots of lower plant life, making it slick and potentially dangerous. Best during low water conditions.

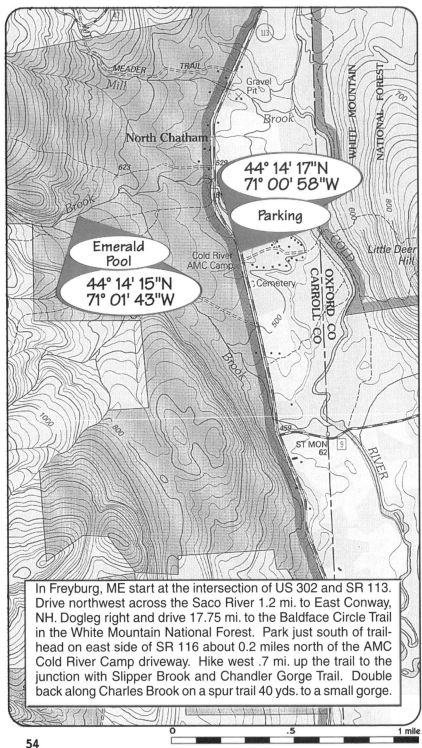

44° 14' 17"N
71° 00' 58"W

Parking

Emerald
Pool

44° 14' 15"N
71° 01' 43"W

In Freyburg, ME start at the intersection of US 302 and SR 113. Drive northwest across the Saco River 1.2 mi. to East Conway, NH. Dogleg right and drive 17.75 mi. to the Baldface Circle Trail in the White Mountain National Forest. Park just south of trailhead on east side of SR 116 about 0.2 miles north of the AMC Cold River Camp driveway. Hike west .7 mi. up the trail to the junction with Slipper Brook and Chandler Gorge Trail. Double back along Charles Brook on a spur trail 40 yds. to a small gorge.

0   .5   1 mile

Emerald Pool

If this doesn't make you want to peel off your laundry and jump right in, then you should surrender your ADK card and spend vacations in Atlantic City.

The swimming hole happens at the top of the Cold River in the White Mountain National Forest where Charles Brook has worked it's way among some bedrock and hogged out a funnel-shaped hole about 20 feet long and easily eight feet deep. The color and clarity of the water rolling off of North Baldface Mountain is startling. Seating is limited, but there's room for a couple of small groups among the hemlock trees adjoining the fall.

Emerald Pool is actually in New Hampshire, but since it's accessed from Freyburg, ME (and there's already an Emerald Pool in New Hampshire) it's reviewed as being part of the great state of Maine. It's less than one mile from the trailhead and a very easy hike. Park just south of the trailhead on the east side of SR 116 about 0.2 miles north of the AMC Cold River Camp driveway. Hike west up the trail to the junction with Slipper Brook and Chandler Gorge Trail. Double back along Charles Brook 40 yds. to a small gorge.

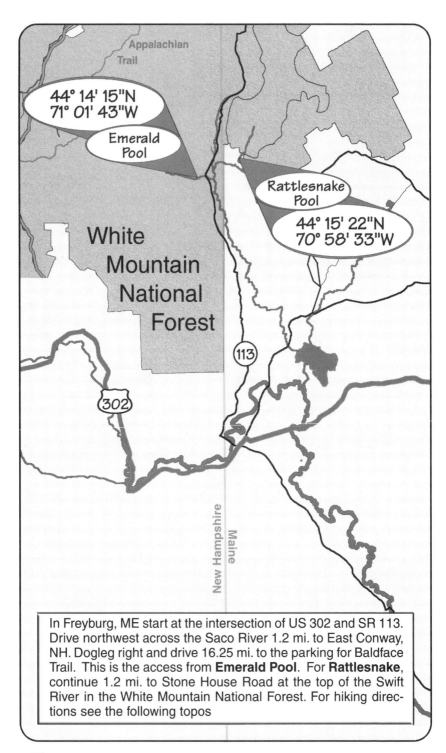

44° 14' 15"N
71° 01' 43"W

Emerald
Pool

Appalachian
Trail

Rattlesnake
Pool

44° 15' 22"N
70° 58' 33"W

White
Mountain
National
Forest

113

302

New Hampshire

Maine

In Freyburg, ME start at the intersection of US 302 and SR 113. Drive northwest across the Saco River 1.2 mi. to East Conway, NH. Dogleg right and drive 16.25 mi. to the parking for Baldface Trail. This is the access from **Emerald Pool**. For **Rattlesnake**, continue 1.2 mi. to Stone House Road at the top of the Swift River in the White Mountain National Forest. For hiking directions see the following topos

Rattlesnake Pool

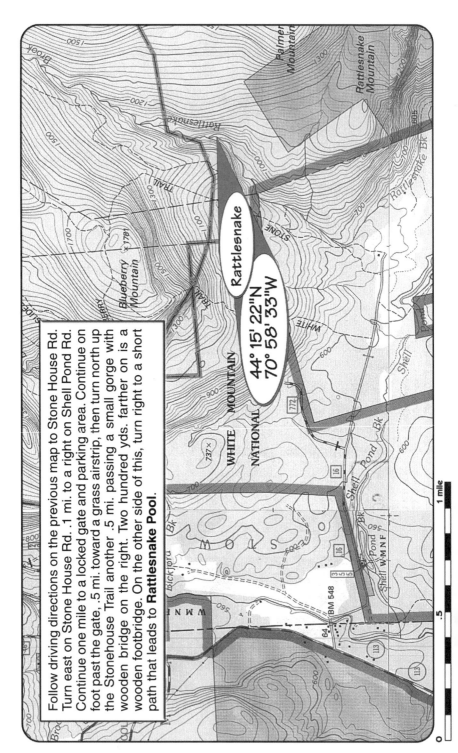

Follow driving directions on the previous map to Stone House Rd. Turn east on Stone House Rd. .1 mi. to a right on Shell Pond Rd. Continue one mile to a locked gate and parking area. Continue on foot past the gate, .5 mi. toward a grass airstrip, then turn north up the Stonehouse Trail another .5 mi. passing a small gorge with wooden bridge on the right. Two hundred yds. farther on is a wooden footbridge. On the other side of this, turn right to a short path that leads to **Rattlesnake Pool.**

Rattlesnake

44° 15' 22"N
70° 58' 33"W

1 mile

.5

Rattlesnake Pool

Water coming out of the Caribou-Speckled Mountain Wilderness is so clean and clear that it seems to have its own luminance. Seriously, I visited in the early evening with light fast receding, but the reflective quality of the water was so magnificent that I could take the photo without a tripod. Especially enjoyable is the short trail that approaches the pool. It's a muffled walk on pine needles until you emerge on a slope above Rattlesnake Brook looking 20 vertical feet down through a woodland setting into a glowing bowl of water.

The fall that helped create the pool is no different from countless woodland cascades in Maine or the White Mountain National Forest. What makes Rattlesnake stand out is that differential weathering caused the water to bore out a hole about the size of a backyard swimming pool. It has a clear bottom of bedrock with a submerged lip of stone downstream that's responsible for the depth of at least nine feet. Some limited shallow dives are fun.

Steep angles limit seating. A ledge to the left of the fall as you look upstream will accommodate a couple and there are other scattered rocks for singles to sit on. Also, too much shade and too many companions. It's less than 20 minutes from the parking area. See the map at left for details. Best visit on a weekday. One final note: Rattlesnake is well loved and well cared for. Keep it like that.

Katahdin Fall

45° 13' 52"N
70° 11' 59"W

On the Appalachian Trail going up Katahdin. No pool at the bottom, though.

Long Falls

45° 08' 01"N
70° 11' 01"W

Dead River just above Flagstaff Lake. I didn't like it that much, but, maybe I was just in a bad mood on the day I reviewed it.

The Tubs

45° 05' 57"N
70° 13' 39"W

On the Appalachian Trail above Carrabassett. Shallow.

Huston Brook

45° 21' 54"N
69° 56' 20"W

A community swimming hole above Carrabassett.

Moxie Fall

44° 44' 58"N
70° 32' 31"W

A good spot 200 yards up from the fall, but lots of litter.

Tumbledown Pond

44° 34' 16"N
70° 54' 23"W

Above Weld, ME. Marginal swimming destination.

Screw Auger Falls

44° 34' 16"N
70° 54' 23"W

Grafton Notch State Park. Shallow basins. Nearby Mother Walker Falls is also a bust.

Step Falls

44° 34' 50"N
70° 51' 47"W

Wight Brook above the Bear River. Numerous pools, but none deep enough to qualify as a swimming hole. Beautiful, though.

Three pools

44° 38' 32"N
70° 35' 17"W

On the Swift River above Rumford, ME. Crowds.

Dunn Fall

44° 39' 41"N
70° 53' 57"W

The Appalachian Trail west of Andover, ME. Too dark and narrow to merit a visit of itself, but great place to pause on the AT.

Bickford Slides

44° 16' 07"N
70° 59' 28"W

The Caribou-Speckled Mountain Wilderness. Maybe I missed it, I didn't find anything remotely interesting.

Keezar Gorge

44° 11' 53"N
70° 48' 54"W

Almost made the cut, but a little too dark and mossy.

New Hampshire
& the
White Mountains

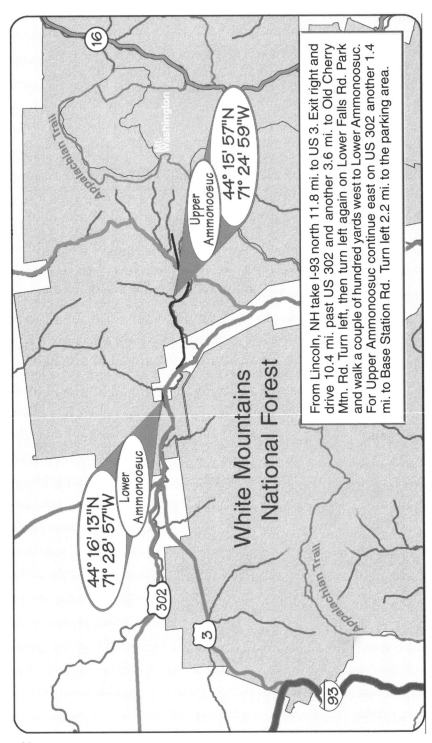

44° 16' 13"N
71° 28' 57"W

Lower Ammonoosuc

16

Appalachian Trail

Mt. Washington

Upper Ammonoosuc

44° 15' 57"N
71° 24' 59"W

White Mountains National Forest

Appalachian Trail

302

3

93

From Lincoln, NH take I-93 north 11.8 mi. to US 3. Exit right and drive 10.4 mi. past US 302 and another 3.6 mi. to Old Cherry Mtn. Rd. Turn left, then turn left again on Lower Falls Rd. Park and walk a couple of hundred yards west to Lower Ammonoosuc. For Upper Ammonoosuc continue east on US 302 another 1.4 mi. to Base Station Rd. Turn left 2.2 mi. to the parking area.

Upper Ammonoosuc

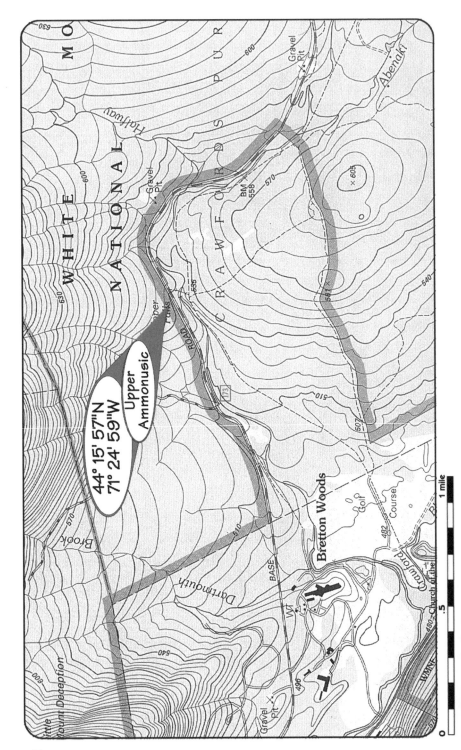

44° 15' 57"N
71° 24' 59"W

Upper
Ammonusic

Upper Ammonoosuc

A couple of roiling potholes below a broad sheet of granite where the sun shines warm and relaxing on long summer afternoons. Ammonoosuc is divided in thirds. The top contains shallow concavities cut in ergonomic contours and buffed smooth by the runoff from Mt. Washington. Below a wooden foot bridge lies the short middle section which is the most photographed part of the fall.

Here, the Ammonoosuc River has augered an audacious kettle of water 10 feet around with walls about 18 vertical feet. (As you look downstream from the bridge, a piece of sculpted granite on the right is reputed to look like a profile of FDR. I thought it looked more like Eleanor.) The pothole below is three times the diameter, not as deep, but with walls of similar height. Water is a clear, mineral green that is begging you, just begging you, to jump in. But wait until you've seen a couple local kids make the leap and get safety pointers from them. You won't have long to wait.

The third portion is about 200 yards below the bridge. It's not the most dramatic feature in the White Mountain National Forest, but much less visited. It's composed of a modest pothole in a narrow constriction. Below the constriction flares into a pool that's fair to good. 'Bout the only place you can escape crowds.

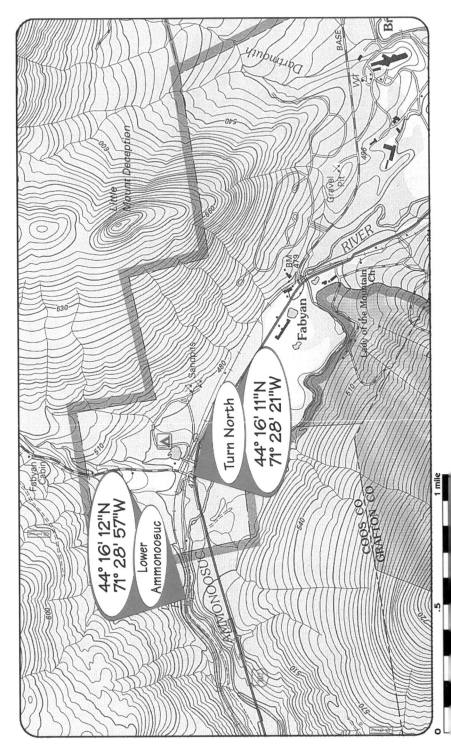

Turn North
44° 16' 11"N
71° 28' 21"W

44° 16' 12"N
71° 28' 57"W
Lower
Ammonoosuc

1 mile

.5

0

Lower Ammonoosuc

Entirely different from Upper Ammonoosuc Fall. This place is so big and round that it seems like a design rather than a natural occurrence. In fact, part of the right bank is a gravel road and some scars in the rock point to earlier industrial use, but the present appearance is largely unspoiled. At the top is a long, low-angle cascade over dozens of individual shelves from couch size to garden size. They separate the water into so many different leaps and falls that it really adds to the character.

The swimming area happens at the bottom of the cascade where a dogleg forces the Ammonoosuc River to swell into a hole big enough for ducks to land in. It's the biggest swimming hole in the White Mountain National Forest and among the biggest swimming holes in this book. The best part is the accessibility. Grandpa can take the kids down here six weeks after his hip surgery while you and the spouse have brunch at Bretton Woods. The Lower Fall is only two tenths of a mile from the parking area. Rocks at the cascade are cut into even angles like stair steps six to nine inches high.

It has at least one killer pothole higher up in the run. It's about the size of a double jacuzzi. Much of the rest of the riverbed above and below has lots more boulder clutter. Few places more than six feet deep, but worth exploring since privacy at the main hole is doubtful.

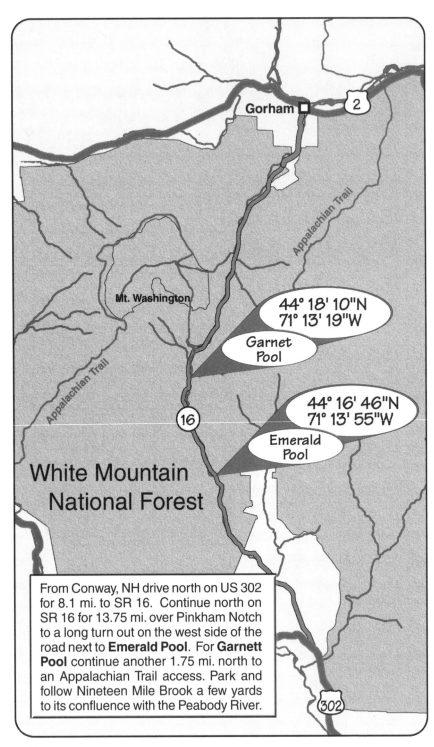

Gorham

2

Appalachian Trail

Mt. Washington

44° 18' 10"N
71° 13' 19"W

Garnet
Pool

Appalachian Trail

44° 16' 46"N
71° 13' 55"W

16

Emerald
Pool

White Mountain
National Forest

From Conway, NH drive north on US 302
for 8.1 mi. to SR 16. Continue north on
SR 16 for 13.75 mi. over Pinkham Notch
to a long turn out on the west side of the
road next to **Emerald Pool**. For **Garnett
Pool** continue another 1.75 mi. north to
an Appalachian Trail access. Park and
follow Nineteen Mile Brook a few yards
to its confluence with the Peabody River.

302

Emerald Pools

I could imagine a better swimming hole in New Hampshire; I just couldn't find one. This spot in the White Mountain National Forest is broad and deep. A ring of rock rises out of the river, making an impound that's about 25 feet wide and 60 feet from the boulders at the bottom to the columns forming the top of the hole.

You wouldn't call the columns twins, but they're very similar in angle, dimension, effect and purpose. Both are nearly vertical and about eight feet tall. They stand seven feet apart, the distal end of a bedrock formation that pinches the river together, accelerating it and producing the erosive force that keeps the pool below clear.

Water quality was good when I visited, with visibility of about six feet. Officials say that it doesn't get the amount of visitors you would imagine, given its easy access. It's beyond view of the road, but unless the water is running, you'll be able to hear the cars whooshing by. Still, you'll find many more people clustered in several less impressive spots along the Kangamangas Highway, just because it's better known. Emerald Pool certainly gets more people than can be accommodated by limited lounging at the top and the smallish, uncomfortable rocks at the bottom.

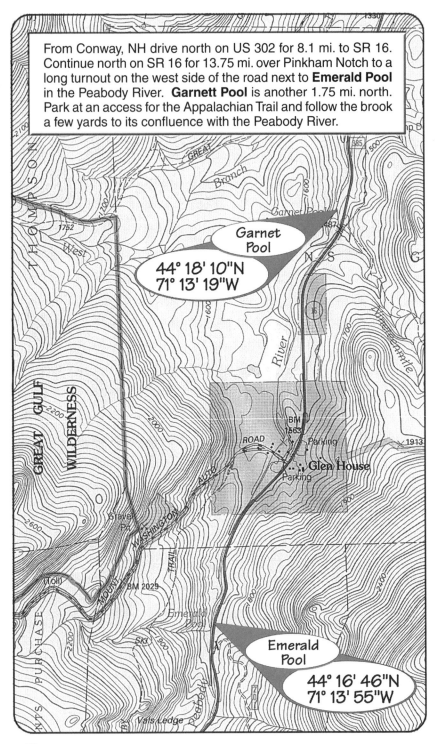

From Conway, NH drive north on US 302 for 8.1 mi. to SR 16. Continue north on SR 16 for 13.75 mi. over Pinkham Notch to a long turnout on the west side of the road next to **Emerald Pool** in the Peabody River. **Garnett Pool** is another 1.75 mi. north. Park at an access for the Appalachian Trail and follow the brook a few yards to its confluence with the Peabody River.

Garnet
Pool

44° 18' 10"N
71° 13' 19"W

Emerald
Pool

44° 16' 46"N
71° 13' 55"W

Garnet Pool

Garnet Pool occurs at a constriction in the Peabody River. It's around 140 feet long and unusably narrow over most of its length before it flares at the bottom into a pool about 12 feet across and 20 feet long. A gravel bank and some ledges permit shallow dives in water that's about eight feet deep in the center. The river points northeast, which is a liability way up north in the White Mountain National Forest.

It will fit a couple of groups. If you spread out a little you'll have some privacy. Best move upstream to a shallow pot with elegantly sculpted rock containing many chutes and channels carved into the stone. It has a better woodland setting than the main pool. There's a great platform for sunning in this upper portion. It will be on the right as you face upstream. In sum, a nice place to retreat and enjoy all the textures and contour of the stone along with some additional privacy.

Water quality is the same as Emerald Pool upstream, which is to say about six feet of visibility with a little bit of sediment. Also, like Emerald, it loses points on surroundings. Although the road isn't visible, it's only 50 yards away.

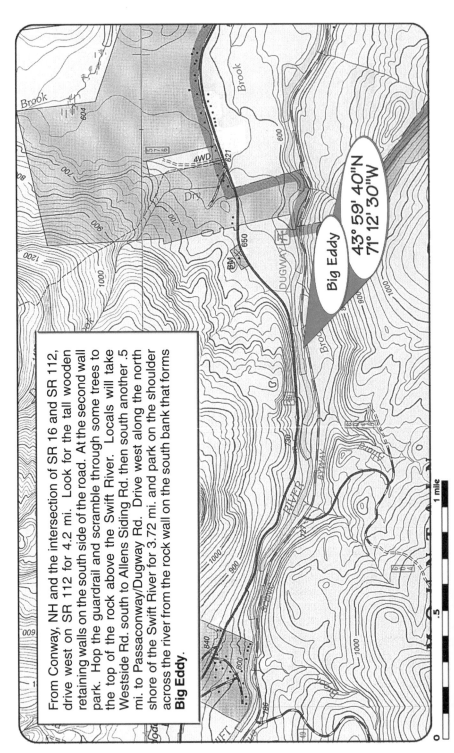

From Conway, NH and the intersection of SR 16 and SR 112, drive west on SR 112 for 4.2 mi. Look for the tall wooden retaining walls on the south side of the road. At the second wall park. Hop the guardrail and scramble through some trees to the top of the rock above the Swift River. Locals will take Westside Rd. south to Allens Siding Rd. then south another .5 mi. to Passaconway/Dugway Rd. Drive west along the north shore of the Swift River for 3.72 mi. and park on the shoulder across the river from the rock wall on the south bank that forms **Big Eddy**.

Big Eddy

43° 59' 40"N
71° 12' 30"W

1 mile

.5

Big Eddy

Looking for a swimming hole on the Swift River is like cruising a singles bar. Eddy isn't the best looking. Not the best body, not even the deepest. What Eddy represents is the lone figure who's your best shot at getting some action without having to compete against the hordes of others looking for fun. The river parallels the Kancamagus Highway, a scenic route that draws tourists to the White Mountain National Forest the way Donna Summer used to fill a disco. There are at least six spots between Lincoln and Conway with campgrounds and rest areas that funnel no fewer than one dozen people into the water on any sunny day.

Eddy is a discreet rock outcrop on the south side of the river beyond the view of passing cars. It's around 15 feet high, a detail that's sort of immaterial because it's difficult to imagine the modest pool beneath getting deep enough to arrest a falling body. The riverbed here is wide and filled with cobble. Nothing to improve the depth — except for that rock. It blocks the accumulation of freestone and leaves a tiny crescent of a swimming hole. During low flow there will be a nice seat at the base of the rock, right at water level.

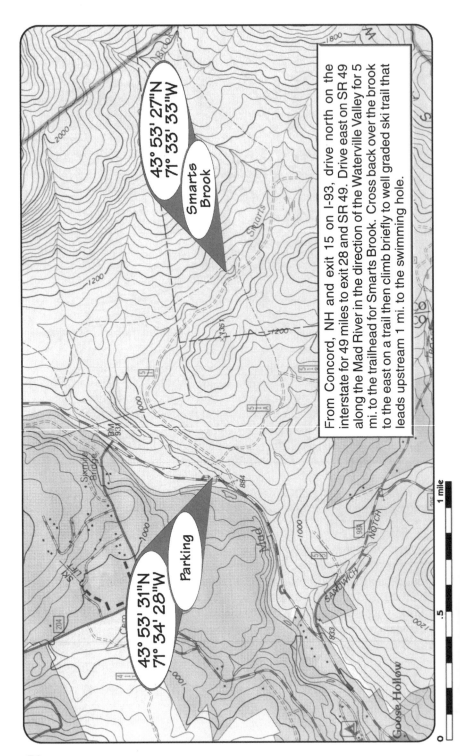

43° 53' 27"N
71° 33' 33"W

Smarts Brook

From Concord, NH and exit 15 on I-93, drive north on the interstate for 49 miles to exit 28 and SR 49. Drive east on SR 49 along the Mad River in the direction of the Waterville Valley for 5 mi. to the trailhead for Smarts Brook. Cross back over the brook to the east on a trail then climb briefly to well graded ski trail that leads upstream 1 mi. to the swimming hole.

43° 53' 31"N
71° 34' 28"W

Parking

Goose Hollow

0   .5   1 mile

Smarts Brook

Water with such magnificent color, that I swooned. Beautiful rock, too. It's a cascade with a shallow pitch that runs about 20 feet over some very solid, unjointed rock. Below lies an unusually symmetrical bowl of turquoise water set in the deep, dark green of a mixed woodland setting. A series of steps/seats, each about 18 inches high march down into the water. They look like stadium seats. The pool is semi-circular in shape, perhaps seven feet deep and about 25 feet wide.

It's a tiny watershed, just over nine square miles, in the Sandwich Range Wilderness of the White Mountain National Forest. That suggests volume may vary considerably. The above photos were taken in autumn during a condition of moderate drought. So it's quite a bit faster and colder earlier in the season when precipitation has been closer to normal. Depth is probably not greatly affected by amount of runoff as there's no impound that would improve the volume of the pool. Velocity may increase considerably, though, making Smarts a potential waterslide.

Access is very mild, given its location along a wide, level trail. And at one mile from the pavement, it's an easy trip for anybody in the family. Several places along the trail are revegetation areas. Do not walk off trail. Do not harvest plants or otherwise damage vegetation.

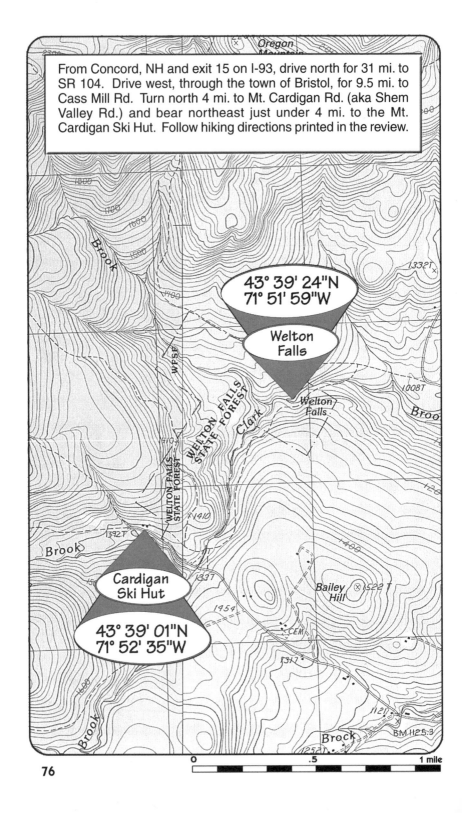

From Concord, NH and exit 15 on I-93, drive north for 31 mi. to SR 104. Drive west, through the town of Bristol, for 9.5 mi. to Cass Mill Rd. Turn north 4 mi. to Mt. Cardigan Rd. (aka Shem Valley Rd.) and bear northeast just under 4 mi. to the Mt. Cardigan Ski Hut. Follow hiking directions printed in the review.

43° 39' 24"N
71° 51' 59"W

Welton
Falls

Cardigan
Ski Hut

43° 39' 01"N
71° 52' 35"W

0   .5   1 mile

Welton Fall

Water that spills off Mt. Cardigan and Orange Mountain collects into the Fowler River which cuts a deep fall in eponymous Welton Falls State Forest. The fall begins at a pronounced rock knob on the south. Below this promontory, water falls into an extremely narrow catch basin with a sheer rock wall rising about 30 feet from the water level. A cable handrail inhibits jumping and prevents a slip over the low side on the steep, wet rock.

The Fowler River continues, spilling into a lower pool that is the main destination. It's an oval about 45 feet long and 15 feet wide at the top. The topography is so narrow, so deeply shaded, that I'll bet the water stays cold all the damn time. Based on its orientation, I don't see it getting any direct sun at all.

From the Cardigan Mountain ski hut, begin at the eastern end (near end) of the parking lot and walk north into a picnic area. Follow signs one mile downstream and cross the stream to the east at a hemlock tree with a double yellow blaze. The trail climbs briefly over a knob and then descends to the fall.

Faults are heavy usership, lack of sun and limited horizontal component to relax on. Also, there's a bunch of graffiti at the top by the fall. Probably collects litter, but it was clean when I visited.

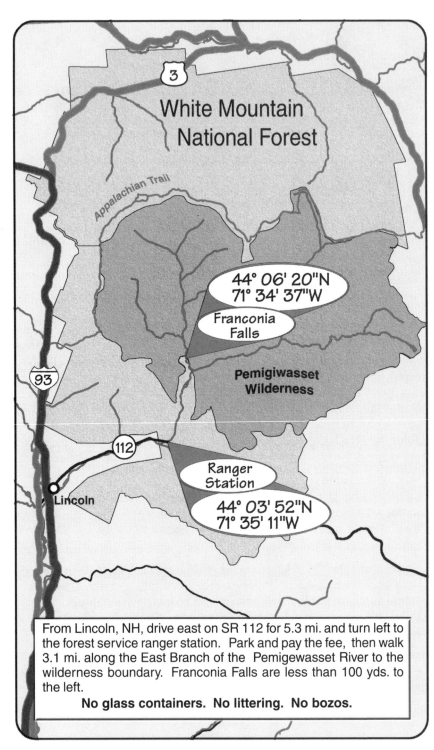

White Mountain National Forest

Appalachian Trail

44° 06' 20"N
71° 34' 37"W

Franconia Falls

Pemigiwasset Wilderness

Ranger Station

44° 03' 52"N
71° 35' 11"W

Lincoln

From Lincoln, NH, drive east on SR 112 for 5.3 mi. and turn left to the forest service ranger station. Park and pay the fee, then walk 3.1 mi. along the East Branch of the Pemigewasset River to the wilderness boundary. Franconia Falls are less than 100 yds. to the left.

No glass containers. No littering. No bozos.

Franconia Falls

A waterpark. Franconia Falls is an expanse of smooth, polished granite with so many dips, lips, chutes, slides and sinkers that, were it not for the fact the water flows downhill, you could get lost for days. Sources say that under optimal conditions you can ride as far as 120 feet before a splash landing in runoff from the Pemigiwasset Wilderness.

The most popular tube is no more than 18 inches wide at the bottom. Apparently the water flows over such a broad expanse of rock that it can't concentrate on hogging out really big holes or wide slides. Nobody can attest to this better than Tom Hyland of Lincoln, NH.

"Granite doesn't have lots of elasticity," he explained. "It's a good size for kids, but if you're an adult you have to turn sideways. I went from a 34 waist to a 32 waist just like that."

It's far from the dumbest thing that's happened at Franconia Falls. The place is such an attraction that the White Mountain National Forest limits the number of visitors. Regulars say that the trail, an abandoned rail grade, can look a sidewalk filled with people. Some of the result is damaged vegetation, fecal coliforms and the general condition of a place too much loved and too little cared for by users.

Gem Pool

44° 16' 00"N
71° 19' 34"W

Fall and basin on the Ammonoosuc Ravine Trail. So high on the western flank of Mt. Washington that water is painfully cold.

Diana's Bath

44° 04' 09"N
71° 10' 30"W

Plush falls and really tasty granite, but pools aren't nearly deep enough.

Lower Falls

44° 00' 55"N
71° 14' 41"W

A slide on the Swift River along the Kancamagus Highway. Fewer people at a Red Sox game.

Cascade Brook

44° 07' 21"N
71° 41' 27"W

Falls & cascades near Pinkham Notch along the Appalachian Trail. Crowds, not much depth.

Sabbaday Falls

43° 59' 35"N
71° 23' 48"W

In the Saco River behind the police station on Conway, NH. Just a big wide river. Nothing too interesting.

Jigger Johnson

43° 59' 40"N
71° 19' 50"W

No deep pools. Nice beaches, though.

The Pool

44° 06' 12"N
71° 40' 36"W

State Route 16 near Pinkham Notch. No Swimming.

Old Hole

44° 02' 51"N
71° 39' 37"W

East Branch Pemigewasset River near Lincoln, NH. Condos visible downstream. Why Bother?

Indian Leap

44° 01' 44"N
71° 43' 02"W

Magnificent rock sculpting, but right behind a restaurant.

Livermore Falls

43° 47' 04"N
71° 40' 02"W

Little more than a wide spot in the river, but one with a tremendous beach and lots of college students. In the Livermore Falls State Forest near Plymouth, NH.

Sculptured Rocks

43° 42' 24"N
71° 51' 21"W

Intriguing rock. Not deep enough.

Vermont
& the
Green Mountains

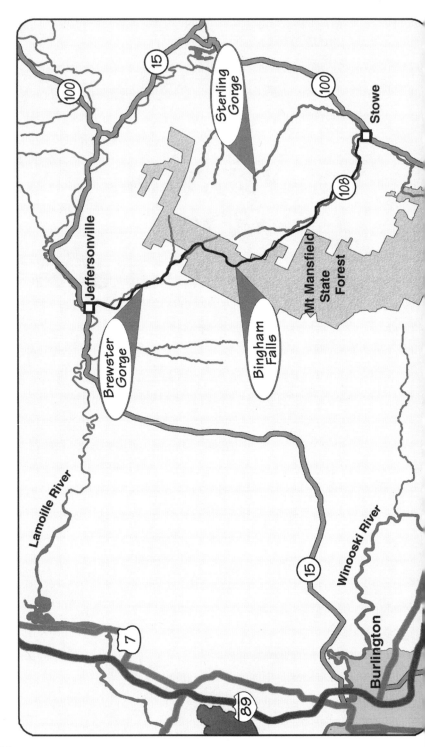

Bingham Falls

From the intersection of SR 100 and SR 108 in Stowe, VT, drive northwest on SR 108 (aka Mountain Rd.) for 6.4 mi. toward Smuggler's Notch. You'll find a wide parking area on the western side of the road. The trail starts on the eastern side of the road and descends .2 mi. to the West Branch of the Waterbury River. Turn right at the top of **Bingham Falls** and descend a short, steep distance to the pool at the bottom. For **Foster's**, start in Stowe, but drive only as far as the village of Stowe Fork. Turn north on Notchbrook Rd. After .3 mi. you come to a second set of guardrails. Park on either end of the guardrail and look for the hole just below the road.

44° 31' 09"N
72° 46' 02"W

Bingham
Falls

44° 30' 22"N
72° 45' 29"W

Foster's

0   .5   1 mile

Bingham
Falls

A Yosemite-class swimming hole; just the sort of thing you'd expect to find in the Sierra backcountry. The hole is approximately 30 feet wide and filled with deep, dark water spilling down from Smugglers Notch. It plunges two stories into a stone amphitheater with moss covered walls 45 feet high. Hemlocks and hardwoods put a canopy over the streambed and help create an even more enclosed space.

You'll find beautifully sculpted rock above the falls. No swimming above the falls, though. People are frequently injured trying to scramble down into it. The informal trail to the bottom of the fall descends 60 vertical feet and is steep enough that a stick is very helpful. Or for balance you could lean on any of the 100 or so people likely to visit on a weekend.

Water quality is generally good, but it may receive sediment from activity at the ski area. Only a couple of good rocks to sit on and not much to dive from. The canyon points southwest, making it more of an afternoon spot. For an overview, cross the stream at the outlet and walk around to the top of the eastern wall.

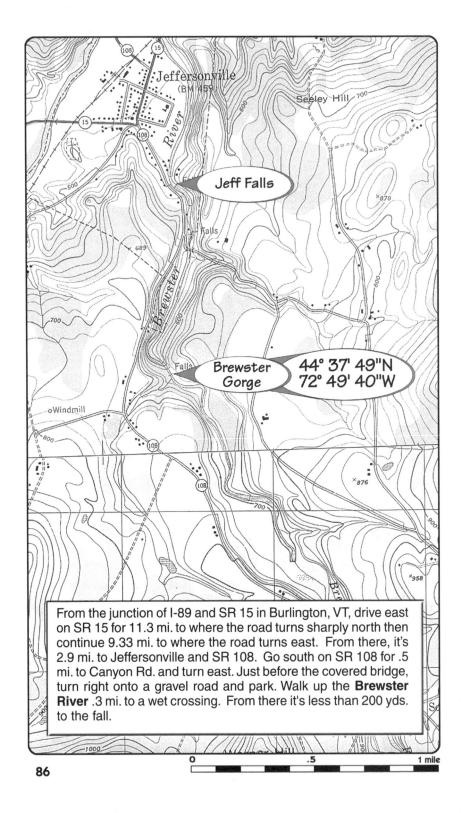

Jeffersonville
(BM 459)

Seeley Hill 700

Jeff Falls

River

Falls

689

Brewster

700

Falls

Brewster
Gorge

44° 37' 49"N
72° 49' 40"W

Windmill

800

108

108

876

700

958

Brewster River

From the junction of I-89 and SR 15 in Burlington, VT, drive east on SR 15 for 11.3 mi. to where the road turns sharply north then continue 9.33 mi. to where the road turns east. From there, it's 2.9 mi. to Jeffersonville and SR 108. Go south on SR 108 for .5 mi. to Canyon Rd. and turn east. Just before the covered bridge, turn right onto a gravel road and park. Walk up the **Brewster River** .3 mi. to a wet crossing. From there it's less than 200 yds. to the fall.

1000

0   .5   1 mile

Brewster Gorge

The Brewster River passes from a floodplain through a steep gorge that has a remote feeling despite its proximity to roads and settlement. At the bottom of the gorge there's a wading pool that stretches around to the left of a camping platform with a heavily used fire ring. From the wading pool the water deepens into something big enough for a few strokes. At the top of the gorge water drops more than 30 feet, plunging into a couple of tight potholes about ten feet wide with gobs of rockfall and snags. The trail to the top of the gorge starts at the fire ring and climbs to the left of the river, but there's no safe descent to the pools on this side of the canyon.

These are all the parts of Brewster to ignore.

Instead, scramble part way up the gorge from the bottom. Amid the more than one dozen boulders, some the size of small houses, the river takes three bounces and lands in a small, deep Jacuzzi with a brilliant seat opposite. Plus, there's a butt-wide ledge at water level so you can kick back and take it all in. There's also room on an adjoining boulder for sunning.

You have to approach from the right. So cross at the bottom of the fall and follow a path uphill about 20 yards. Couple of tricky steps among the boulders to get down to this place. Nothing serious, though.

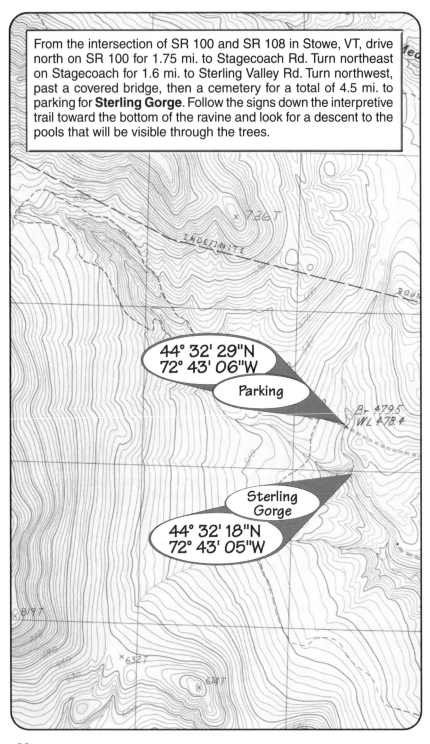

From the intersection of SR 100 and SR 108 in Stowe, VT, drive north on SR 100 for 1.75 mi. to Stagecoach Rd. Turn northeast on Stagecoach for 1.6 mi. to Sterling Valley Rd. Turn northwest, past a covered bridge, then a cemetery for a total of 4.5 mi. to parking for **Sterling Gorge**. Follow the signs down the interpretive trail toward the bottom of the ravine and look for a descent to the pools that will be visible through the trees.

44° 32' 29"N
72° 43' 06"W

Parking

Sterling Gorge

44° 32' 18"N
72° 43' 05"W

Sterling Gorge

Two pots and a pan. Sterling Brook contains more than one dozen falls and cascades along a ravine that's about 400 feet long. Walls are less than 30 feet tall, though not continuous. The rock is bedded at 50 degrees to the flow of water and that's what creates the several cascades. The best pools are at the bottom of the gorge, two steep sided potholes and one broad, flat bottomed pool with low sides. This series of three begins with the top pothole, 20 feet wide and 15 feet long.

Owner Gar Andersen says that he's jumped into it, about six vertical feet. The launch is from a collar of rock, but you have to get some clearance because there's a hunk of rock that's fallen in at the downstream end. The more difficult part is getting out. It's surrounded on nearly 360 degrees by sheer rock. The only break in the rock is for the discharge. It tumbles another seven feet or so into an even narrower cauldron. Then that empties via a four-foot fall out into a broad, boulder and cobble filled pan of water, about 20 or 30 feet on the main axis. It probably gets chin deep at the sweet spot. A flake of schist like a king size bed is flopped right at the bottom of the pool. Not like the bed at home though. People passing on the nature trail above are within sight.

There's a good parking area and a small trail maintained by the Sterling Falls Gorge Natural Area Trust. The trail begins just after a footbridge.

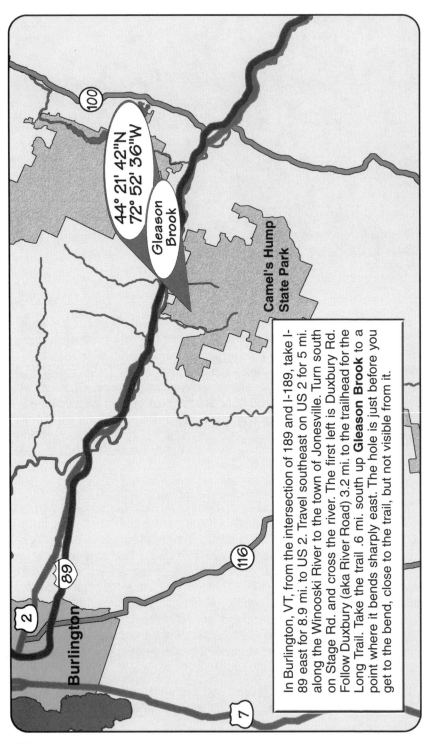

44° 21' 42"N
72° 52' 36"W

Gleason Brook

Camel's Hump State Park

Burlington

In Burlington, VT, from the intersection of 189 and I-189, take I-89 east for 8.9 mi. to US 2. Travel southeast on US 2 for 5 mi. along the Winooski River to the town of Jonesville. Turn south on Stage Rd. and cross the river. The first left is Duxbury Rd. Follow Duxbury (aka River Road) 3.2 mi. to the trailhead for the Long Trail. Take the trail .6 mi. south up **Gleason Brook** to a point where it bends sharply east. The hole is just before you get to the bend, close to the trail, but not visible from it.

Gleason Brook

44° 21' 42"N
72° 52' 36"W

WINOOSKI

RIVER

WINOOSKI

VERMONT

CENTRAL

BM
346

Wiley Lodge

GREEN MOUNTAINS

LONG TRAIL

Brook

Gleason

THE LONG TRAIL

0   .5   1 mile

Gleason Brook

Gleason is a funnel-shaped pool in a nice slice of bedrock. It's a small brook most people pass on the way to Camel's Hump. A flume runs 100 linear feet and empties into a pool about 25 feet long. Solid rock sides slope upward for 15 to 25 feet, but the best part is the rock at the discharge. It's a flake tilted vertically to create a tremendous impound. That's what's responsible for the depth.

The spur trail that leads to the pool is unmarked. You can, however, discern the cascade from the trail. It's about 40 vertical feet below the foot trail and looks like a white smudge in the dark forest. If water levels are higher, you can hear it also. The best tip is that the spur is just below a three-way fork. To continue on the main trail you would bear left. Walking straight leads less than 100 yards to an informal camping area. The spur trail is on the right and descends steeply for a short distance.

Don't come here expecting to take a nap. Horizontal space is limited and there are only a couple of places to sit. Much of the rock is moss covered; the rest of it's very slick. Lots of beech trees create too much shade.

Bonus Feature: from the trailhead, before you cross the wooden footbridge, turn downstream. Bushwhack about 250 yards to a set of cascades. At the bottom is a little pool about chest deep. Very private.

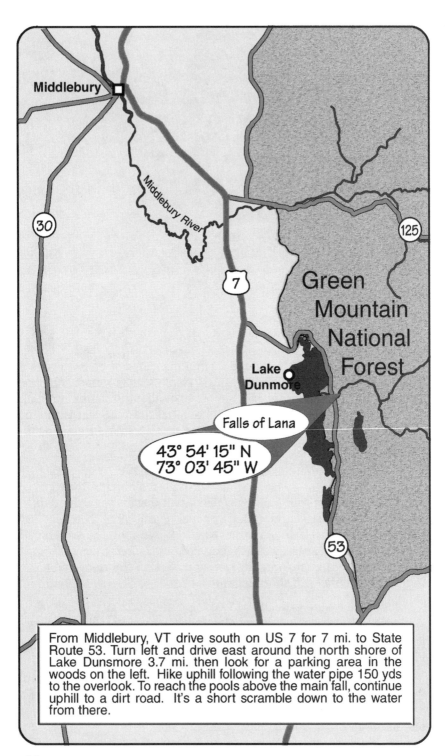

Middlebury

30

Middlebury River

7

125

Green Mountain National Forest

Lake Dunmore

Falls of Lana

43° 54' 15" N
73° 03' 45" W

53

From Middlebury, VT drive south on US 7 for 7 mi. to State Route 53. Turn left and drive east around the north shore of Lake Dunsmore 3.7 mi. then look for a parking area in the woods on the left. Hike uphill following the water pipe 150 yds to the overlook. To reach the pools above the main fall, continue uphill to a dirt road. It's a short scramble down to the water from there.

Falls of Lana

Hurry. Sometime during the next 1,000 years this may turn into nothing more than a rocky cascade. Between the pool at the top and the main fail, the water is forced into a natural flume that traverses the rock face at a 90-degree angle to the fall line. It's caused by a narrow rock fin less than four feet high. Very unusual and once it's breached the water will likely run too fast to pool.

Follow map directions to the penstock, a large pipe that diverts water into the generating station below. Once you're on the dirt road perpendicular to the penstock you'll easily find the uppermost cascade. It's about 15 feet high and after bouncing around some, it enters a pool about 35 feet long. It's obstructed by some boulders, but deep enough. Descent into the pool is a little bit treacherous. From the top, look left for a gully descending through trees. Follow it to a rock face 30 feet high, then angle farther left toward a cleft in the rock that runs the length of the face and descend.

Once at the fringe of the pool there's plenty of horizontal space, but since the rock is bedded vertically there's nothing comfortable to sit on, except for one seat five feet wide and covered with sand. It's right at the top of the flume. The ravine faces west. That means afternoon sun will shine warm and buttery on your face.

Borderline classic, but high visitorship. Unless you're comfortable descending on toeholds and hand holes, avoid this.

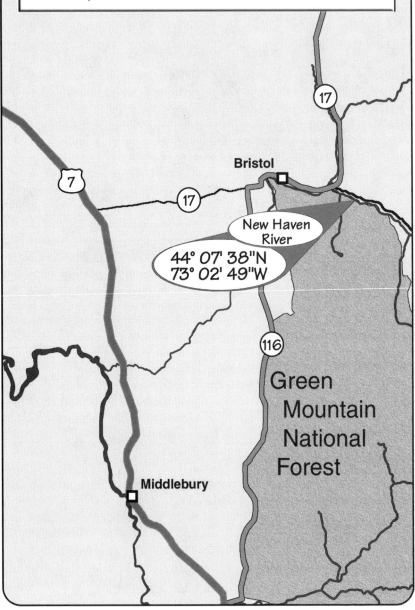

From Middlebury, VT drive north on US 7 for 8 mi. to SR 17. Drive east on SR 17 for 6.9 mi. through the town of Bristol, across the **New Haven River** and make an immediate right on Lincoln Gap Road. The hole is .25 mi. from here. There is another popular, but less notable hole, located 1.4 mi. upstream from the junction of Lincoln Gap Rd. and SR 17.

Bristol

New Haven River

44° 07' 38"N
73° 02' 49"W

Green
Mountain
National
Forest

Middlebury

New Haven River

You will find three swimming holes at the bottom of the New Haven River. You will also find a significant portion of the local population between the ages of 12 and 25. The river is a wide mountain stream with a boulder filled channel through most of its course until it reaches some Cambrian quartzite, a very old, and hard rock that tends to fracture in blocks.

The uppermost swimming hole is 1.4 miles from the village of Rocky Dell. Here, a massive ledge of quartzite lies tilted in the middle of the river. It's the most amazing sunning slab. There are some pools and cascades around it, but they pale compared to the hawg hole downstream. The hole is fed by an attractive fall five or six feet high that rolls over an undercut ledge in a near perfect curtain of water.

It's a small gorge with tall ledges of the aforementioned quartzite pointing into the deep end of a pool that is 40 feet wide and at least twice as long. The ledges are ten to 15 feet above the water and have enough frontage on the water that you and twelve of your friends could link arms and jump at the same time.

It's all very impressive and certainly qualifies as a classic until you factor in the number of visitors and the amount of trash, including broken glass.

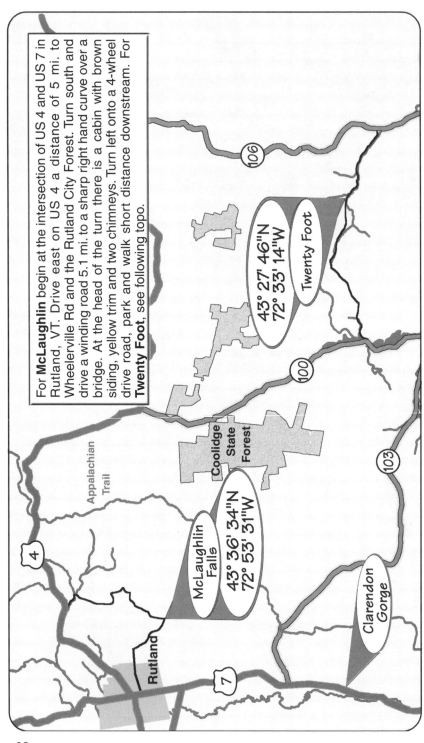

For **McLaughlin** begin at the intersection of US 4 and US 7 in Rutland, VT. Drive east on US 4 a distance of 5 mi. to Wheelerville Rd and the Rutland City Forest. Turn south and drive a winding road 5.1 mi. to a sharp right hand curve over a bridge. At the head of the turn there is a cabin with brown siding, yellow trim and two chimneys. Turn left onto a 4-wheel drive road, park and walk short distance downstream. For **Twenty Foot**, see following topo.

Twenty Foot

43° 27' 46"N
72° 33' 14"W

106

100

103

Coolidge State Forest

McLaughlin Falls

43° 36' 34"N
72° 53' 31"W

Appalachian Trail

4

Rutland

7

Clarendon Gorge

McLaughlin Fall

A gorgeous fall on North Branch Creek. It's a woodland setting 100 steps from a dirt road. Great sense of enclosure with rock as high as 35 feet wraps 120 degrees around the water. There's a steeply overhanging face on the right as you look upstream. The left side is the head wall containing the lip of the fall. Water has down cut deeply into the rock creating a notch about one yard wide. This is what accounts for the beauty of the fall; the water shoots out in one smooth torrent that plunges into a square-shaped pool with a cobble and sand bottom. Because of all the rock fall it's relatively shallow, not much better than seven feet deep. Birches produce heavy shade in the summer.

The fall faces southeast, directly opposite a sand beach that's approximately 100 square feet, depending on water level. Water is very dark, but not at all cloudy. It glows olive green with the sun shining straight into it. Although there are a couple of cabins immediately above, all the rest of the watershed is mountain stream. I rate the water quality as excellent.

Given the "No Swimming" throughout the Rutland City Forest it would seem impossible to find a swimming hole along this road. McLaughlin, however, is outside the city forest, so you can peel off those sticky trousers and hop right in. Please note there's evidence that this is a party spot. Some broken glass at the parking area.

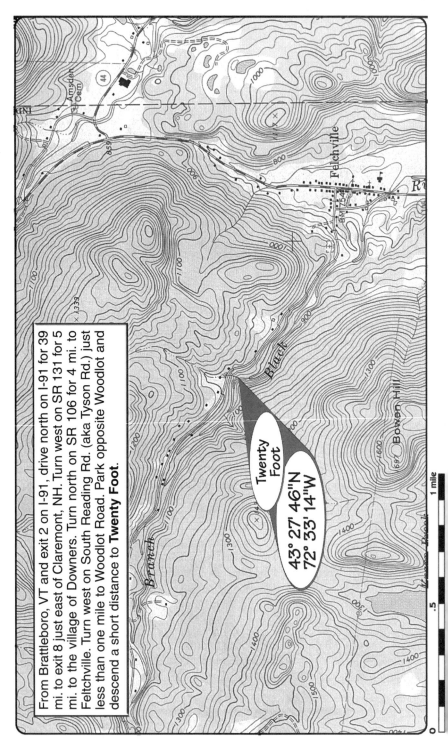

From Brattleboro, VT and exit 2 on I-91, drive north on I-91 for 39 mi. to exit 8 just east of Claremont, NH. Turn west on SR 131 for 5 mi. to the village of Downers. Turn north on SR 106 for 4 mi. to Feltchville. Turn west on South Reading Rd. (aka Tyson Rd.) just less than one mile to Woodlot Road. Park opposite Woodlot and descend a short distance to **Twenty Foot**.

Twenty Foot

43° 27' 46"N
72° 33' 14"W

.5

1 mile

Twenty Foot

The North Branch of the Black River cuts through a patch of evergreen and down into some highly folded rock. The walls are moderately undercut, deeply contoured and scarcely 15 feet apart at the broadest. It's a premier low water spot because it's so tight, anything other than low levels will be awfully fast. Water is beautiful and clear.

Bennett Hammond grew up in nearby Brownsville. Forty years and countless cigarettes later, he found himself lying in a Boston hospital bed recovering from quadruple bypass and thinking about Twenty Foot.

"We'd jump off the highest place you could, the 20-foot jump where you couldn't even see the water. Jumping from that height where you can't see the water, even though you know it's there. You could call it a metaphor for life."

Ten months after his surgery, Hammond decided to revisit this part of the river to renew his faith for the first time since he was 16.

"It's just a miracle that it hasn't been ruined," he said toweling off.. "A miracle that it hasn't been changed. The trees are a little thicker around the middle, but so are we all."

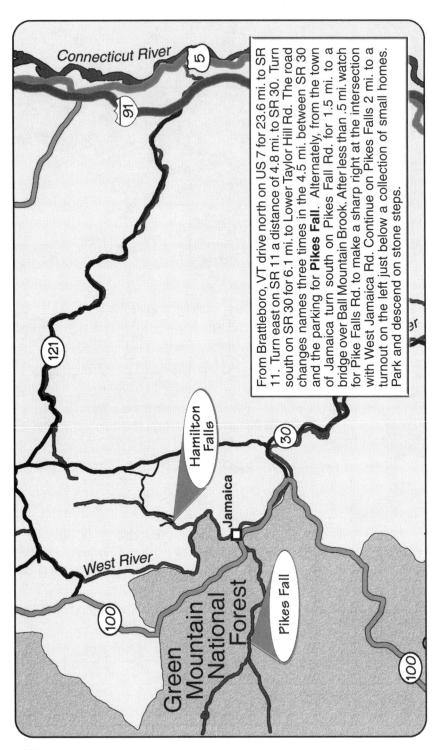

From Brattleboro, VT drive north on US 7 for 23.6 mi. to SR 11. Turn east on SR 11 a distance of 4.8 mi. to SR 30. Turn south on SR 30 for 6.1 mi. to Lower Taylor Hill Rd. The road changes names three times in the 4.5 mi. between SR 30 and the parking for **Pikes Fall**. Alternately, from the town of Jamaica turn south on Pikes Fall Rd. for 1.5 mi. to a bridge over Ball Mountain Brook. After less than .5 mi. watch for Pike Falls Rd. to make a sharp right at the intersection with West Jamaica Rd. Continue on Pikes Falls 2 mi. to a turnout on the left just below a collection of small homes. Park and descend on stone steps.

Pikes Falls

Pikes Falls happens where Ball Mountain Brook butts up against a belly full of Precambrian rock. It's a huge ledge of quartzite that creates some cool hydraulics. Water descends into a narrow channel and splits into three cascades with the highest being about seven feet. The rock collects the water again into an intermediate tub, then punches it through a narrow chute that spills into the main pool.

The pool measures about 40 feet from the cascade to the discharge and is perhaps 10 feet at its deepest. There's simply too much cobble clutter to create a hole that's deep throughout. The water quality is good. Runoff from the eastern flank of Stratton Mountain enters just above the fall. It's clear and pure. No turbidity when I visited. However, there are lots of cabins and small holdings in the northern part of the watershed.

The best part isn't the water at all, but the bedrock. It's several hundred square feet of rock that faces east. You can bring the whole birthday party down here. It's going to be warm all the time except when it's overcast and rainy.

Pikes Falls is a community swimming hole administered by the city of West Jamaica. It gets heavy local use, but appears well cared for. It's open dawn to dusk. No camping. No fires. No motorized vehicles. No littering. No altering natural vegetation.

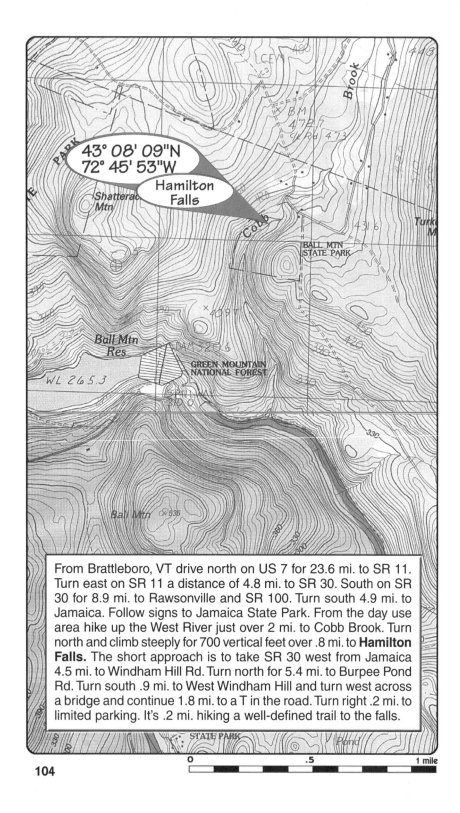

43° 08' 09"N
72° 45' 53"W

Hamilton
Falls

From Brattleboro, VT drive north on US 7 for 23.6 mi. to SR 11. Turn east on SR 11 a distance of 4.8 mi. to SR 30. South on SR 30 for 8.9 mi. to Rawsonville and SR 100. Turn south 4.9 mi. to Jamaica. Follow signs to Jamaica State Park. From the day use area hike up the West River just over 2 mi. to Cobb Brook. Turn north and climb steeply for 700 vertical feet over .8 mi. to **Hamilton Falls.** The short approach is to take SR 30 west from Jamaica 4.5 mi. to Windham Hill Rd. Turn north for 5.4 mi. to Burpee Pond Rd. Turn south .9 mi. to West Windham Hill and turn west across a bridge and continue 1.8 mi. to a T in the road. Turn right .2 mi. to limited parking. It's .2 mi. hiking a well-defined trail to the falls.

0 .5 1 mile

Hamilton Fall

Hamilton is a steep, woodland cascade with pools above and below. The bedrock is schist tilted at about a 20-degree angle to the flow of Cobb Brook. The main feature is at the top, a pothole 25 feet across and 15 feet deep. There's a consistent nine feet of water in it due to a steep lip that creates a beautiful impound. Below, the water slips over a high-angle rock face and runs 20 feet to another pothole that's very dangerous to reach and really not worth the effort. Water leaves that intermediate pot and runs another 25 feet or so to some modest, more user-friendly bathtubs at the bottom.

Access to the top pot is via a ladder bolted into the rock. If you jump in you can get eight to ten feet of vertical. Before the ladder was installed the only way out of the sheer sided hole was a delicate traverse of the fall lip. That's how injuries happened. Joanna Western of Burlington grew up at an adjacent boarding school that her parents owned.

"My parents would go down in the gorge to keep a victim warm and calm until the rescuers arrived," she said. "The first time I saw a cadaver I was barely a teenager."

All of which is to say, use caution.

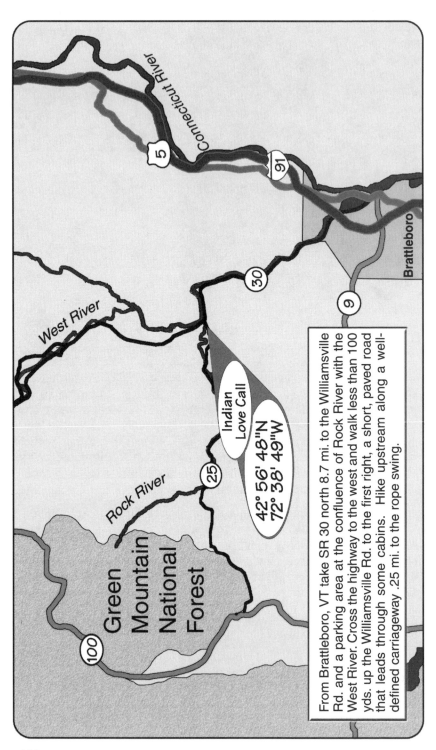

Indian
Love Call

42° 56' 48"N
72° 38' 49"W

From Brattleboro, VT take SR 30 north 8.7 mi. to the Williamsville Rd. and a parking area at the confluence of Rock River with the West River. Cross the highway to the west and walk less than 100 yds. up the Williamsville Rd. to the first right, a short, paved road that leads through some cabins. Hike upstream along a well-defined carriageway .25 mi. to the rope swing.

Indian Love Call

Long sand beach with a good jumping rock and clean, clear water. The current is slight, the bottom sandy. Overlooking the hole is a hemlock parkland backing a broad sand beach. It can be as long as 120 feet, depending on water level. The jumping rock opposite the beach is 12 feet high. For those who need more height, one of the trees has boards nailed to it in ladder fashion so you can get an extra eight feet of whoopee. Because the Rock River is low altitude, it warms up earlier than most. The downside is that a ridge blocks afternoon sun.

Love Call is popular with the cognoscenti. While most people driving north from Brattleboro go to the West River for summer fun, those in the know walk the other way up the Rock River. Will Hutchinson is lessee of the property on State Route 30 where the parking is.

The lowest hole, the one with the beach opposite the trail, is private. Love Call is generally a family spot, he said. The hole above and around the bend is mixed gender, clothing optional. The pools above that are generally gay, said Hutchinson.

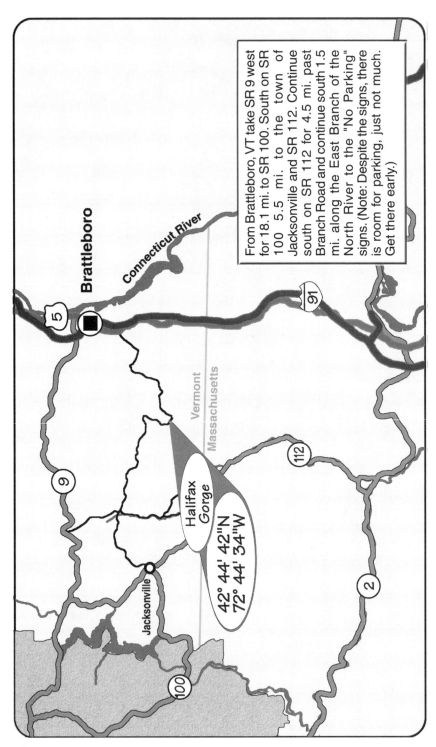

Brattleboro

Connecticut River

Vermont

Massachusetts

Halifax
Gorge

42° 44' 42"N
72° 44' 34"W

Jacksonville

From Brattleboro, VT take SR 9 west for 18.1 mi. to SR 100. South on SR 100 5.5 mi. to the town of Jacksonville and SR 112. Continue south on SR 112 for 4.5 mi. past Branch Road and continue south 1.5 mi. along the East Branch of the North River to the "No Parking" signs. (Note: Despite the signs, there is room for parking, just not much. Get there early.)

Pro Tour

Pro Tour

Halifax Gorge

The premier late season spot in southern Vermont. The entire gorge occupies 120 yards on the East Branch of the North River. Here is the inventory: rope swing, jumping ledges, small sand beach, clean water, sunny rocks, and deeply shaded evergreen banks.

At the top is a deep bowl flanked by conifer parkland. Below, the gorge narrows with as little as six feet separating walls as tall as 20 feet. Loads of sculpted rock in the serpentine-shaped channel. The walls relax a little and make room for the primary jumping spot.

At the bottom of the gorge is the main hole. It's more than 80 feet long and deep throughout. In addition to the small sand beach that holds four to five people, there is a flat-sided boulder about 10 feet square and numerous other two and three-seat rocks all around. The river runs generally east to west. That means it will get good sunlight throughout the day. Even at the low level I surveyed, the water was moving, not icky, not sticky.

Lots of visitorship, much of it from students at Marlboro College. Many "No Parking" signs. The area at the top of the gorge will hold about one dozen cars. I'm sure it gets more than that, to judge from the chipmunks grown fat on Cheetos, Fritos and Doritos. Nevertheless, local groups periodically pick up discarded snack wrappers.

Hippie Hole

44° 53' 56"N
72° 38' 54"W

West Hill Brook outside Montgomery, VT.

Three Holes

44° 52' 32"N
72° 34' 37"W

The Trout River east of Montgomery Center, VT.

Gibou Road

44° 51' 06"N
72° 36' 51"W

South Branch near Hectorville, VT. Not a hiking destination, but good if you want to swim under an historic covered bridge.

Four Corners

44° 56' 12"N
72° 24' 32"W

Community swimming hole beside State Route 101 in Bugbee Brook.

Rock Point

44° 29' 32"N
73° 14' 56"W

Burlington, VT in North Beach Park. Lots of people dip in Lake Champlain here. Not something you'd cross state boundaries to visit, though.

Sheep's Hole (aka Journey's End)

Three little features on Foot Creek near Johnson, VT. Small and within a settled area.

Moss Glen Falls

44° 28' 55"N
72° 37' 26"W

In the Putnam State Forest near Stowe, VT. An 80-foot cascade, but the pool at the bottom was insignificant.

Jeff Falls

44° 38' 25"N
72° 49' 36"W

Just south of Jeffersonville, VT in the Brewster River, right beside State Route 108. Given the number of better places available, this one is a pass.

Bolton Potholes

44° 22' 38"N
72° 52' 29"W

Several fabulous deep pools. Rowdy and littered when I visited. Lots of broken glass.

Preston Brook

44° 22' 08"N
72° 54' 27"W

Very pretty, small gorge on the Long Trail. Several pools and good vertical. However, the best pool will likely be no more than chest deep.

Huntington Gorge

44° 14' 05"N
72° 58' 06"W

Bozo factor is off the charts. Really heavily visited because the rock sculpting and diving is exquisite, but the location along a road, coupled with the number and quality of visitors make this a "why bother" spot.

Lower Middlebury Gorge

43° 58' 13"N
73° 05' 08"W

Popular spot favored by locals and students from Middlebury, VT. It's right under the bridge on State Route 125, though.

Twin Bridge

43° 46' 40"N
72° 42' 02"W

River swimming in the White River near Gaysville, VT. Right along State Route 107. Twin Bridge is nearby.

Warren Falls

44° 05' 39"N
72° 51' 49"W

Major rock sculpting. The pool at the bottom is a good 12 feet deep pool and colorful, but that doesn't tell the whole story. Tests for fecal coliforms do. Way too many idiots.

The Punchbowl

44° 08' 54"
72° 50' 33"W

A clothing optional spot in the Mad River less than three miles north of Warren, VT. Little more than a big sand beach on a wide, flat river. Locals report that it's favored by older gentlemen "of a certain orientation."

Clarendon Gorge

43° 30' 58"N
72° 57' 55"W

The Mill River has a too popular spot near Clarendon, VT. Great water features, but dozens of people in a summer day.

Swinging Bridge

43° 31' 12"N
72° 55' 31"W

The Mill River has another spot, this one 2.5 miles upstream from US 7 on the Appalachian Trail below East Clarendon. Good stop if you're through hiking the AT.

Brockaway Gorge

43° 12' 23"N
72° 30' 50"W

A big deep gorge in the Williams River below a train trestle. Water has an odor.

Little Egypt

Saxtons River outside of Bellows Falls, VT. Way too much nasty stuff upstream.

Buttermilk Falls

43° 26' 11"N
72° 43' 42"E

A family spot on Branch Brook above Ludlow, VT.

Cavendish Gorge

43° 22' 52"N
72° 35' 53"W

A little-known spot in the Black River downstream from Ludlow, VT. Probably worth a visit.

Quechee Gorge

43° 38' 02"N
72° 24' 34"W

Tourist spot know as Vermont's Grand Canyon. The Ottauquechee River can get dirty. Crowded, too.

Dorset Quarry

A popular community swimming hole at an abandoned marble quarry in Dorset, VT.

Button Fall

43° 23' 35"N
73° 13' 27"W

Mettawee River in west-central Vermont. One of the prettiest falls I've seen, but thousands of dairy cattle upstream.

The Ledges

A popular clothing optional spot in Harriman Reservoir outside of Jacksonville, VT.

Adirondack
High Peaks

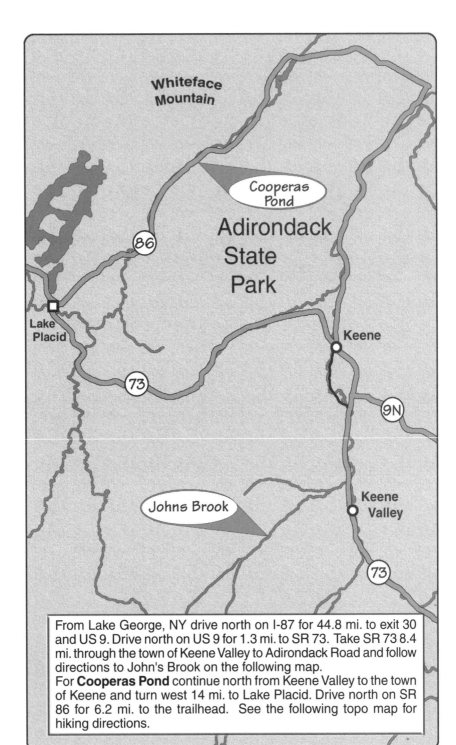

Whiteface
Mountain

Cooperas
Pond

Adirondack
State
Park

86

Lake
Placid

Keene

73

9N

Johns Brook

Keene
Valley

73

From Lake George, NY drive north on I-87 for 44.8 mi. to exit 30 and US 9. Drive north on US 9 for 1.3 mi. to SR 73. Take SR 73 8.4 mi. through the town of Keene Valley to Adirondack Road and follow directions to John's Brook on the following map.
For **Cooperas Pond** continue north from Keene Valley to the town of Keene and turn west 14 mi. to Lake Placid. Drive north on SR 86 for 6.2 mi. to the trailhead. See the following topo map for hiking directions.

Pro Tour

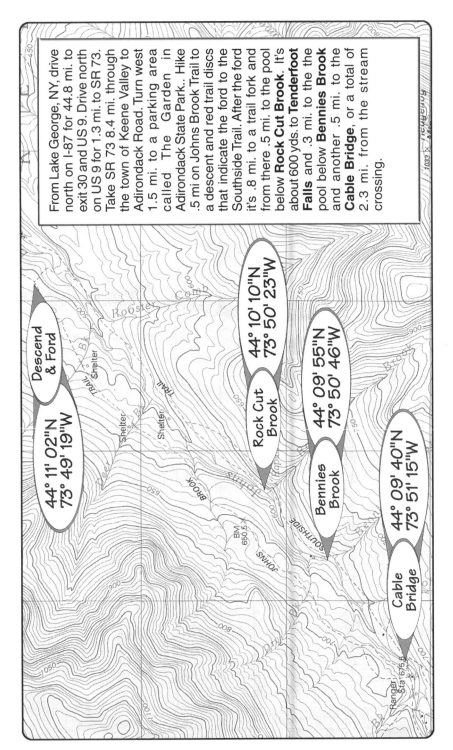

From Lake George, NY, drive north on I-87 for 44.8 mi. to exit 30 and US 9. Drive north on US 9 for 1.3 mi. to SR 73. Take SR 73 8.4 mi. through the town of Keene Valley to Adirondack Road. Turn west 1.5 mi. to a parking area called The Garden in Adirondack State Park.. Hike .5 mi on Johns Brook Trail to a descent and red trail discs that indicate the ford to the Southside Trail. After the ford it's .8 mi. to a trail fork and from there .5 mi. to the pool below **Rock Cut Brook**. It's about 600 yds. to **Tenderfoot Falls** and .3 mi. to the the pool below **Bennies Brook** and another .5 mi. to the **Cable Bridge**, or a total of 2.3 mi. from the stream crossing.

Descend & Ford

44° 11' 02"N 73° 49' 19"W

Rock Cut Brook

44° 10' 10"N 73° 50' 23"W

Bennies Brook

44° 09' 55"N 73° 50' 46"W

Cable Bridge

44° 09' 40"N 73° 51' 15"W

Rock Cut

Two swimming holes along a fisherman's trail on Johns Brook in Adirondack State Park. The upper is the more attractive, the lower is longer and deeper. At the top, a rocky cascade achieves some depth where the current strikes a truck sized boulder fallen into the stream. It creates a sweet spot six to ten feet deep that's about the size of a dinner table. Excellent. Rock on the south side is 15 feet high. The north side has a big block of rock also, but it's much less vegetated and closer to water level. A good place to enter and exit or to enjoy the sun.

Sixty yards below is a hole that's deeper and longer, about 60 feet. It's not as attractive, though. The wall on the north bank is a little more relaxed with good seating, but no access to the water 'cept a jump into a small sweet spot that requires about 10 feet of clearance to avoid clipping rocks on the way down. Some bushwhacking required, but otherwise not especially difficult to reach and lightly visited.

Follow directions on the map to the indicated trail fork. If you go right, you'll be on the fisherman's trail that runs for .4 mi right along the creek to a cross-tie box constructed for trail support. The hole is just beyond. Alternately, stay left at the fork and take the Southside Trail to Rock Cut Brook. The upper hole is 100 yards below Rock Cut's confluence with Johns Brook. Tenderfoot Falls is 800 feet upstream.

Pro Tour

Bennies Brook

Ledges zigzag on both sides of a hole 60 feet long. Only about half of it is swimmable, though. The downstream half is filled in with sand and cobble. The upstream half has excellent depth, but several small boulders obscure the bottom and keep the hole from being deep and continuous.

The best part is the rock. The southern ledges rise as high as nine feet above the creek, but the lower, northern ledge is more attractive and user friendly. It's sunnier and that inhibits moss, lichen and all the lower botany, leaving cool, bare rock to sit on. It's also got excellent access to the deep end.

The cascade above the swimming hole is unremarkable, but above the cascade are extensive slabs of hard rock. Not water slide-able, but a very open and comfortable place to hang out. It's within view of Southside Trail; however, there's a nice picnic area on the north bank, just beyond view of the falls that adds some privacy.

Water quality in all of Johns Brook is excellent. Not the tannic murk common in Adirondack State Park. Expectation of privacy is good. You may want to visit here in the unlikely event that Tenderfoot is crowded.

Pro Tour

Tenderfoot Falls

Water rolls in a gorgeous sheet, thin and continuous over a broad surface of smooth rock. There's enough room to host a wedding reception. Finally, the water rushes toward the center of the creek and into a chute that sends a rooster tail hollering into the main pool. All of which adds up to Adirondack State Park's most popular water slide. The main chute is wide enough for a 40-inch waist. The pool itself is pretty fair. It's wide like the cascade that feeds it with a small deep end right under the rooster tail. At the top of the slide is a really nice pothole, six feet deep and twice as long. Other smaller potholes abound.

Continue walking the streambed about 100 yards to a pair of cascades falling over wide ledges. They are short plunges that come down in three pieces. They land on slabs and exits through a notch and into a slightly larger pool about 25 feet in diameter.

I like this place more and more each time I visit. Finding it the first time can be challenging. Picking up the Southside Trail from the ford of Johns Brook may require some route finding. Look for a red trail disc, then turn right on an old haul road. Very muddy in spots. After the second stream crossing start looking for the slides.

Cable
Bridge

Swimming holes below the cable bridge. Good quality, but not the size of places lower on Johns Brook. The fall comes down in a couple of steps into water that's around 10 feet deep. A ledge about nine feet high stands over a narrow sweet spot. The best way to reach the hole is not directly from the bridge. Rather, 100 yards downstream on the southern bank, look for a bushwhack to the swimming hole. Lots of traffic crossing the foot bridge into the high country, not all of it human.

At The Garden I parked next to a couple of guys coming down from the High Peaks. They were taking off their packs when one of them looked up the trail and said to his friend, "There he is! Hurry up, get in the car!" Standing at the top of the trail was a small, black and white goat scanning the parking lot.

The goat was a mascot for the ADK branch. When his owner joins the group for trail maintenance in Adirondack State Park, the goat comes along. It had wandered off for several days before he fastened onto these two hikers.

"We gave him some peanut butter last night, and some toothpaste this morning. He followed us all the way down the trail," the hiker said through a crack in his car window. "He's very persistent."

The attendant at the parking lot phoned the owner and he was reunited with his goat.

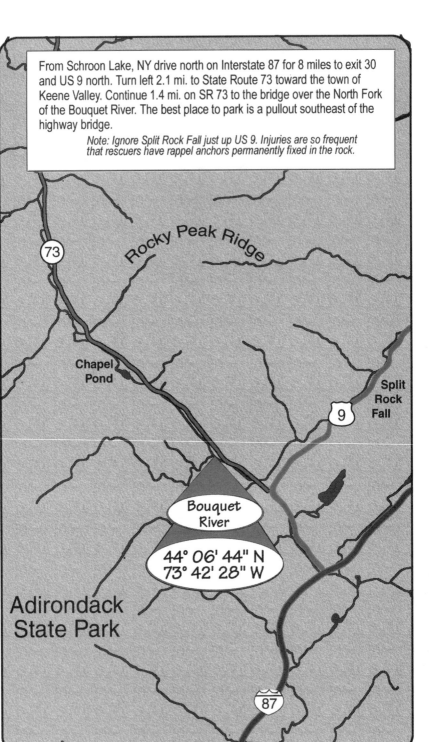

From Schroon Lake, NY drive north on Interstate 87 for 8 miles to exit 30 and US 9 north. Turn left 2.1 mi. to State Route 73 toward the town of Keene Valley. Continue 1.4 mi. on SR 73 to the bridge over the North Fork of the Bouquet River. The best place to park is a pullout southeast of the highway bridge.

Note: Ignore Split Rock Fall just up US 9. Injuries are so frequent that rescuers have rappel anchors permanently fixed in the rock.

Rocky Peak Ridge

73

Chapel Pond

Split Rock Fall

9

Bouquet River

44° 06' 44" N
73° 42' 28" W

Adirondack State Park

87

Bouquet River

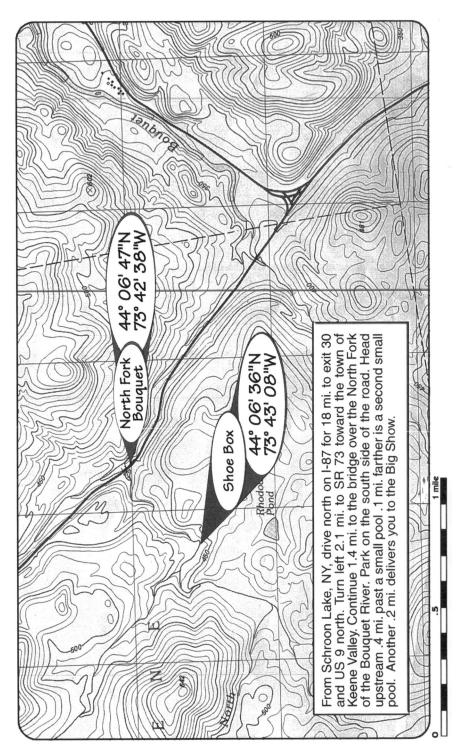

North Fork Bouquet

44° 06' 47"N
73° 42' 38"W

Shoe Box

44° 06' 36"N
73° 43' 08"W

From Schroon Lake, NY, drive north on I-87 for 18 mi. to exit 30 and US 9 north. Turn left 2.1 mi. to SR 73 toward the town of Keene Valley. Continue 1.4 mi. to the bridge over the North Fork of the Bouquet River. Park on the south side of the road. Head upstream .4 mi. past a small pool .1 mi. farther is a second small pool. Another .2 mi. delivers you to the Big Show.

Shoe Box

One big wad of rock put smack in the middle of the North Fork of the Bouquet River. The water, rather than going around the obstacle, barrels through it by means of a gap that's miraculously aligned on the precise axis of the river's flow. Viewed from the top, it's a pile of rock 15 feet with a chimney through which water drops ten feet into a spectacular hole.

The sides are straight and square as a shoe box. Depth is at least 12 feet throughout. The downstream side is a ledge that's been undercut by several feet. Above it, the water rolls out of the hole over an impossibly smooth slab that distributes a perfectly even carpet of silver rolling toward the main stem of the river. Sunning slabs are 55 feet wide and so smooth that I was able to take a nap on bare rock. The only minus is that you're likely to find a couple of other groups from Adirondack State Park visiting here on a summer weekend.

Some lesser places downstream. A nice pool a little more than 600 yards from the trailhead and a better spot 100 yards farther on with a smooth knob that slopes toward the afternoon sun. Good sand beach, too. Water's just about six feet deep during good conditions. Also a smashing hole right above the stone highway bridge where you park, but far too heavily visited. Two even better ones below the bridge with jumps 15 feet high.

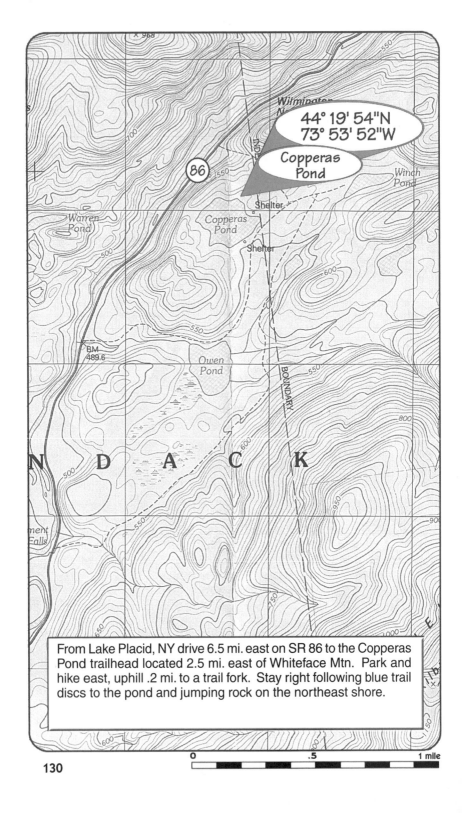

44° 19' 54"N
73° 53' 52"W

Copperas
Pond

From Lake Placid, NY drive 6.5 mi. east on SR 86 to the Copperas Pond trailhead located 2.5 mi. east of Whiteface Mtn. Park and hike east, uphill .2 mi. to a trail fork. Stay right following blue trail discs to the pond and jumping rock on the northeast shore.

0   .5   1 mile

Cooperas Pond

Come for the rock jump; stay for the amphibians. The pond is an easy trip from Lake Placid. It's about 300 yards wide and almost perfectly round, so you can see any part of the lake from any other part. That reduces privacy further at an already popular destination. Visibility is no better than six feet. Good rock structure at many points along the shoreline means you can spread out, although most activity is concentrated at the jumping rock on the north end. It's around seven feet high, an ideal scale for kids who find it fun, not scary.

In between trips from the top of the rock, the kids I interviewed enjoyed catching tadpoles – big tadpoles. One just beginning to get rear legs was four inches across! Conditions in Adirondack State Park during the summer of 1996 so favored amphibian reproduction that regulars said they were big enough to water ski on.

The trail is short but steep. As a guideline, I'd say it's limited to people who smoke no more than one pack a day. Privacy is unlikely. I found 10 people on a cloudy weekday. The area seemed well picked up and cared for.

Note: it's pronounced simply "Cooper's Pond."

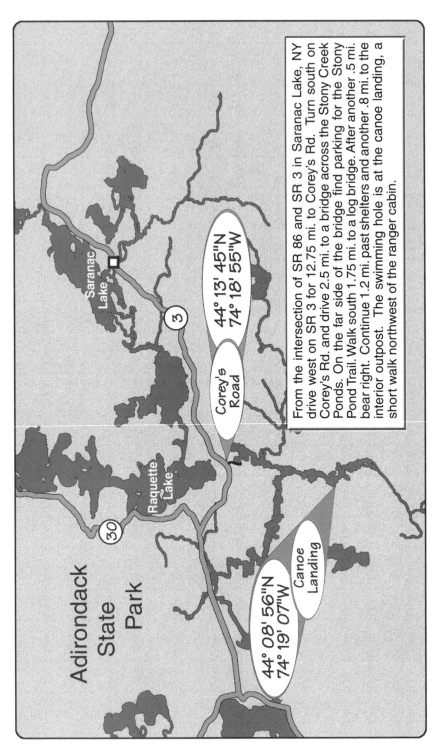

From the intersection of SR 86 and SR 3 in Saranac Lake, NY drive west on SR 3 for 12.75 mi. to Corey's Rd. Turn south on Corey's Rd. and drive 2.5 mi. to a bridge across the Stony Creek Ponds. On the far side of the bridge find parking for the Stony Pond Trail. Walk south 1.75 mi. to a log bridge. After another .5 mi. bear right. Continue 1.2 mi. past shelters and another .8 mi. to the interior outpost. The swimming hole is at the canoe landing, a short walk northwest of the ranger cabin.

Adirondack State Park

Saranac Lake

Raquette Lake

Corey's Road

44° 13' 45"N
74° 18' 55"W

Canoe Landing

44° 08' 56"N
74° 19' 07"W

Raquette River

This is a slackwater spot that's a popular canoe landing with a huge sand beach near the ranger outpost. The river bed here is wide and rock filled. What's exceptional are a couple of large rocks within a small cove. The smaller one splits the river's flow and drives it toward the larger rock where it wraps around the base. Kids favor this spot for low altitude cannon balls. The jump is around 10 feet.

Ben Woodard is Adirondack State Park labor supervisor at the interior outpost nearby. He tends the grounds surrounding what was a backcountry hotel until the 50s. "There used to be lots of different gardens," he explained, "mint, oregano, rhubarb. There's also lots of milkweed. Monarch migrate here in the fall. There's easily an acre of butterflies."

Reports are that during dryer levels there's a nice jacuzzi near the trailhead at the Lower Fall, but it's best to avoid this chute unless you know the river intimately. The Upper Fall is pretty, but too forceful to jump in. There's an eddy south of the fall that might not drag you immediately to your death, but is still dangerous.

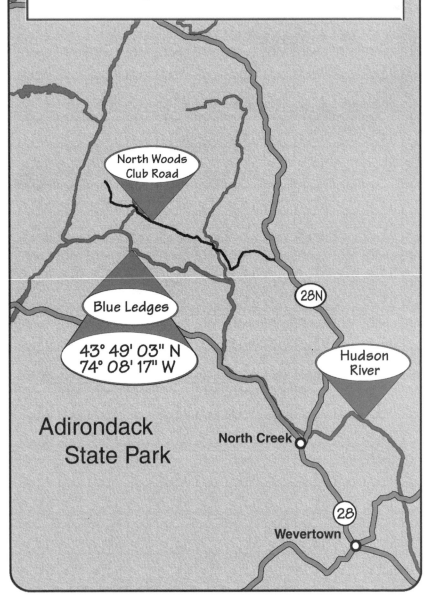

From Lake George, NY take US 9 north for 9 mi. to SR 28. Go north on SR 28 16.3 mi. to the town of North Creek. Turn right onto SR 28N for 9.45 mi. to North Woods Club Rd. Turn left 6.5 mi. on North Woods Club Rd. to Huntley Pond and the trailhead. Descend southwest following blue trail discs .65 mi. to an unnamed creek, cross a foot bridge then climb 200 feet. Turn east .5 mi. then begin a 300-ft descent to the river.

North Woods Club Road

Blue Ledges

43° 49' 03" N
74° 08' 17" W

28N

Hudson River

Adirondack State Park

North Creek

28

Wevertown

Blue Ledges

Here starts what's arguably the finest five miles of the Hudson River. Lightly forested rock walls rise as much as 200 feet above the river at the very top of the Hudson River Gorge in Adirondack State Park. A sharp bend creates a relaxed arc running 200 feet immediately above the gorge with rapids named "Big Nasty" and "Gunsight." Dick Lilliston and his family have visited Blue Ledges annually from the time they had to carry their daughters down to the river in pack baskets.

"Rafters come around the bend dressed in all their trim and tackle, outfitted for class five rapids. The guides have been giving instructions about all the hazards ahead. By the time they round the bend upriver, they're gripping those paddles with white knuckles. And what's the first thing they see? A family placidly backstroking across the Hudson River."

The pools along with the sand beach are great big and can absorb lots of people. Good thing, too. You'll likely encounter lots of kids from nearby summer camps. I even found a couple of cars at a trailhead on a weekday with rain threatening. Trail conditions are apt to be very muddy.

Bonus Feature: Ospreys reside on the ledges above the river.

From Lake George, NY take I-87 north 36 mi. to exit 29 and Boreas Road. Drive west on Boreas Rd. (aka 2B) for 14.9 mi. to Lower Works Rd. Turn north on Lower Works 1.2 mi. to CR 25 (aka Tahawus Rd.) Turn north on Tahawus Rd. 5.8 mi. past the turn off for the village of Tahawus. Continue north, now on Upper Works Rd., for 3.5 mi. to parking for the Upper Works trailhead. From the Upper Works trailhead walk .1 mi. north across a wooden bridge to a trail jct. Bear right toward Lake Colden following red trail discs .9 mi. along **Calamity Brook** to a cable bridge. The pool is visible below the bridge. See following the Opalescent River topo map for hiking directions to upper destinations.

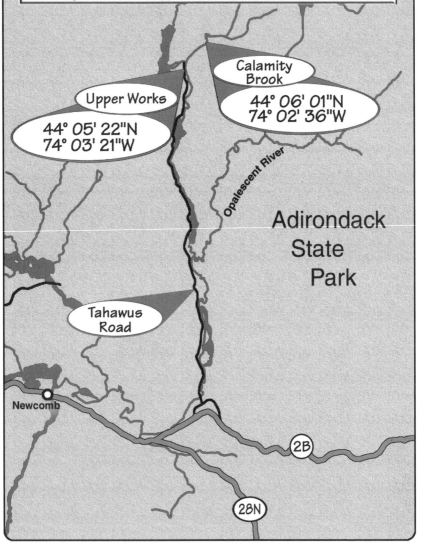

Calamity Brook
44° 06' 01"N
74° 02' 36"W

Upper Works
44° 05' 22"N
74° 03' 21"W

Opalescent River

Adirondack State Park

Tahawus Road

Newcomb

2B

28N

Calamity Brook

Short trip, small dip. A cable footbridge leading to the High Peaks from the west has a couple of nice falls with small pools adequate for rinsing off the mud. Above the bridge water travels over a solid ledge of rock about six feet high. Just before the lip the rock has been dished out, creating several nice, small rooster tails and potholes three to four feet deep.

The swimming spot is below the bridge. It has a shorter fall than upstream, but the bottom broadens into a basin. Boulders clutter the streambed and inhibit the pool depth, but there is an open spot five to six feet deep and ten feet square. You're not likely to find privacy, but Calamity Brook is a good place to freshen up on your way down from the high country. That way you don't have to drive home with the windows rolled down to endure the odor produced by several days of sweating through trails in Adirondack State Park.

The hike up follows red trail discs through unbelievable trail erosion and compaction. Some tree roots are more than 12 inches above the surface. Lots of corduroy, lots of rocks, from suitcase size to steamer trunk. At first it seems like an annoyance until you realize that were they not there you might be walking through serious mud. All the high stepping and weaving means you'll actually be covering more distance than if it were a smooth dry trail, so the hike is more tiring than the map would suggest.

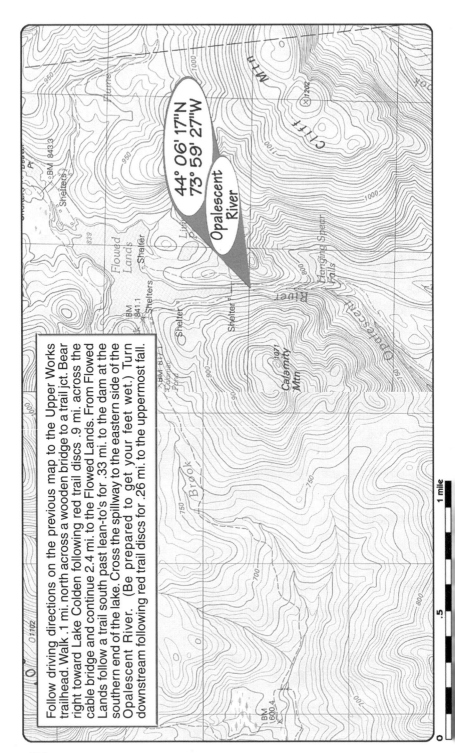

Follow driving directions on the previous map to the Upper Works trailhead. Walk .1 mi. north across a wooden bridge to a trail jct. Bear right toward Lake Colden following red trail discs .9 mi. across the cable bridge and continue 2.4 mi. to the Flowed Lands. From Flowed Lands follow a trail south past lean-to's for .33 mi. to the dam at the southern end of the lake. Cross the spillway to the eastern side of the Opalescent River. (Be prepared to get your feet wet.) Turn downstream following red trail discs for .26 mi. to the uppermost fall.

44° 06' 17"N
73° 59' 27"W

Opalescent River

Opalescent River

The Opalescent River is simply a string of pearls draped over the left shoulder of Adirondack State Park. What the Boquete River is to the eastern slope of the wilderness, the Opalescent is to the western slope. At this hole, a high-angle cascade enters via a stream five feet wide and breaks into hundreds of fractures as it comes stair-stepping down into a kidney shaped hole that's around 40 feet wide. Distance between the face and outlet is 12 to 15 feet. In the middle of the channel are some medium-sized boulders, possibly fracture block that formed the lip of an earlier, higher fall that was undercut and broken off. The fracture block splits the water and forms about the only place you could sit and relax.

Steep ledges on the east (trail side) prevent direct access to the swimming hole. Rather, you must descend from the trail at the outlet of the pool and cross to the western side of the river where it's more user friendly. Careful not to wash over the downstream end. The water can be fast and violent. A good practical measure would be that if you can't cross the log dam at the bottom of Flowed Lands without getting your ankles wet, this place may be too dangerous.

No really luxurious seating on the western side. Nothing to dive from either. Best place to park and enjoy the south facing canyon are the boulders in the middle of the river. Water will be comparatively warm since Flowed Lands collects lots of solar energy, but still best to consider this a late season spot.

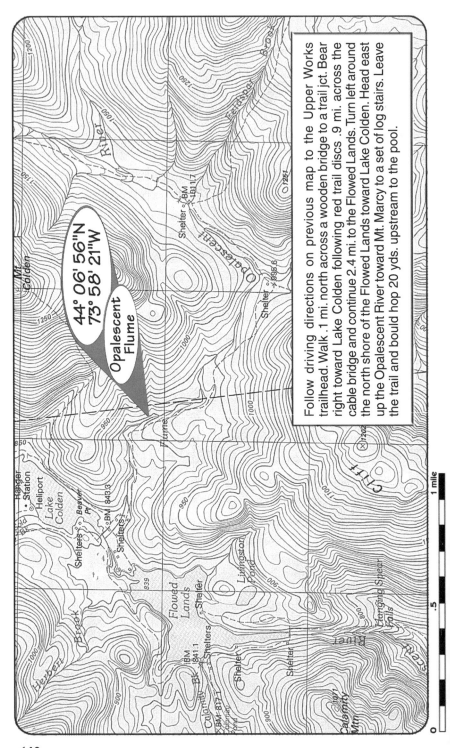

44° 06' 56"N
73° 58' 21"W

Opalescent Flume

Follow driving directions on previous map to the Upper Works trailhead. Walk .1 mi. north across a wooden bridge to a trail jct. Bear right toward Lake Colden following red trail discs .9 mi. across the cable bridge and continue 2.4 mi. to the Flowed Lands. Turn left around the north shore of the Flowed Lands toward Lake Colden. Head east up the Opalescent River toward Mt. Marcy to a set of log stairs. Leave the trail and bould hop 20 yds. upstream to the pool.

Opalescent Flume

The Flume is actually an abyss, a crack that swallows the Opalescent River in a chasm 25 feet deep and barely more than six feet wide at the bottom. Jump into this and you'd be ground into cat food. However, there's a good to fair pool at the bottom. Rather than climb the log steps that parallel the flume, turn into the river and boulder hop 20 yards upstream. You'll find a pool about 20 feet long and one-third as wide. You can recognize it from the sheer, solid wall on the right as you look upstream. Depth is marginal and there is no place to sit, but it has the merit of being the highest practical place to submerge in the headwaters of the Hudson River.

It's far from the only place you can jump in the Hudson headwaters. On the way to The Flume you pass another spot on the Opalescent near a cable footbridge. The pool below the bridge is about as deep as the one below the flume, but the surroundings are more attractive, very open and sunny. Very heavily traveled, though. Just about anyone visiting Adirondack State Park and hiking to Mt. Marcy will pass through here.

Fish Rock

44° 00' 57"N
74° 09' 09"W

West of Camp Santononi on Newcomb Lake. Worth a visit, though not a review.

Duck Hole

44° 08' 32"N
74° 06' 25"W

At the top of the Cold River. Plain ol' lake swimming.

Long Lake

43° 59' 52"N
74° 23' 36"W

A nice beach on east side, just north of Polliwog Pond drainage. Also, numerous islands with sandy beaches, but motor boats kind of ruin it.

Buttermilk Falls

43° 54' 53"N
74° 29' 03"W

Drive up spot on the Raquette River. Marginal pools.

Moody Falls

44° 18' 41"N
74° 42' 55"W

A pile of rocks on the Raquette River. Lots of Plant glop.

Jamestown Falls

44° 19' 29"N
74° 42' 56"W

Too far down the watershed. Poor water quality.

The Pulpit

44° 18' 42"N
73° 58' 05"W

A rock jump on Lake Placid. Motor boats. Yuk!

Marcy Dam

44° 09' 30"N
73° 57' 04"W

Small lake on the Ausable River. First stop for campers heading to the high country.

Avalanche Lake

44° 07' 57"N
73° 58' 08"W

Breathtaking from a distance. Unremarkable up close.

High Falls

44° 20' 58"N
73° 52' 24"W

On the West Branch Ausable. Too many people.

The Flume Falls

44° 18' 40"N
73° 54' 55"W

Ditto.

Monument Fall

44° 07' 33"N
73° 39' 13"W

Mainly a fishing place opposite Owen Lake trailhead.

Split Rock Falls

44° 21' 59"N
73° 50' 25"W

So many injuries that rescuers have rappel anchors permanently bolted into the rock.

Susquehanna
Headwaters

From Williamsport, PA take US 15 north for 12.5 mi. to SR 14. Continue north 11.5 mi. to the town of Ralston. Turn east on Thompson St. and after the second intersection, dogleg left for .5 mi. to the intersection with McIntyre Rd. Continue straight, into Tiadaghton State Forest on Rock Run Rd. for .3 mi. to a parking turnout above **Lover's Rock**. It's another 1 mi. to **First Fall** and **Third Fall** is another 1.6 mi. farther up.

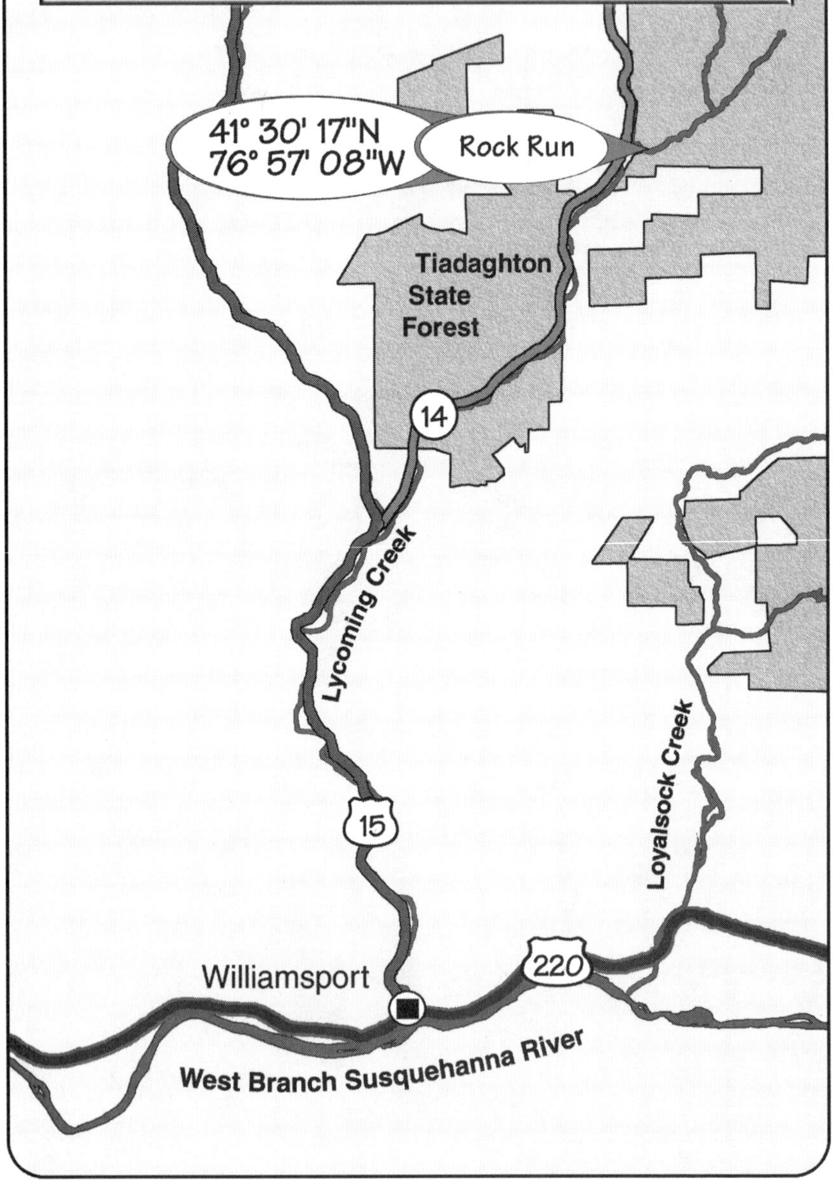

41° 30' 17"N
76° 57' 08"W

Rock Run

**Tiadaghton
State
Forest**

14

Lycoming Creek

Loyalsock Creek

15

220

Williamsport

West Branch Susquehanna River

Lower
Rock Run

First Fall is an improbably long and impossibly deep hole that had an added feature — several speckled trout, one of them was big enough to saddle and ride like a pony. I could not believe there are such big fish in a place so regularly visited. Every ten minutes or so another one of them would take a run at the fall before flopping back into the tank below.

A magnificent rock shelf lines most of the pool's 80 foot length, giving you a six foot step off into some astonishing water with a tremendous emerald color. It's a minimum eight feet deep at the bottom of the fall, but gets really deep below, where water has scooped something that's scuba deep. The only drawback is that once you jump in from the ledge above, you have to swim around to the bottom and walk a short distance back to the top.

Entry and exit is less of a problem one mile downstream where a low, flat ledge forms a teenage makeout spot called Lover's Rock. There's no sign saying as much, so I had to ask around to learn the name. I stopped at the bank and described the place to a couple of tellers. Both women said they knew the place, but to make sure we were talking about the same spot, they began describing how to get there. Confusion ensued and as we were trying to sort it out, another employee stepped in.

"They're just a little mixed up," he said. "Whenever they went it was dark."

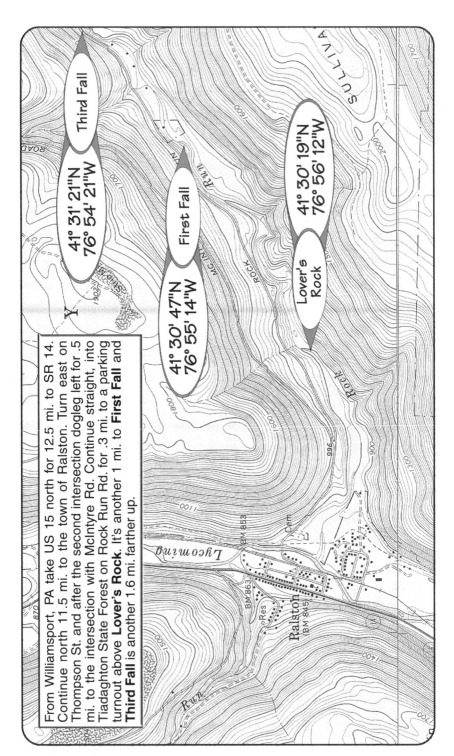

From Williamsport, PA take US 15 north for 12.5 mi. to SR 14. Continue north 11.5 mi. to the town of Ralston. Turn east on Thompson St. and after the second intersection dogleg left for .5 mi. to the intersection with McIntyre Rd. Continue straight, into Tiadaghton State Forest on Rock Run Rd. for .3 mi. to a parking turnout above **Lover's Rock**. It's another 1 mi. to **First Fall** and **Third Fall** is another 1.6 mi. farther up.

Third Fall

41° 31' 21"N
76° 54' 21"W

First Fall

41° 30' 47"N
76° 55' 14"W

Lover's
Rock

41° 30' 19"N
76° 56' 12"W

Upper
Rock Run

The upper fall on Rock Creek comprises three features that add up to one classic swimming hole. At the top, a cascade about seven feet high comes through a single notch in a tiny gorge. Differential weathering has undercut the rock by several feet and produced a triangular hole about 20 feet wide and 35 feet from top to bottom. It's a small watershed, just over 20 square miles, but it produces enough runoff that the water's velocity keeps the ample freestone piled up at the bottom of the pool, leaving the center deep and clear.

Below, Rock Run exits over finely bedded rock whose successive layers have the look of corduroy. Water rolls some 55 feet, narrowing into a chute two feet wide before dropping into a pothole. From there it continues another 10 feet to a shallow basin that marks the end of the run.

Just a little more than one-half mile downstream is the second fall. It's directly behind one of the several private cabins within the Tiadaghton State Forest. It may seem like you're recreating on private property, but you do have legal right to pass. Problem is that second fall isn't really worth the effort. It's really just a low-pitch cascade with a basin at the bottom that is little more than six feet deep. Lots of sun, though.

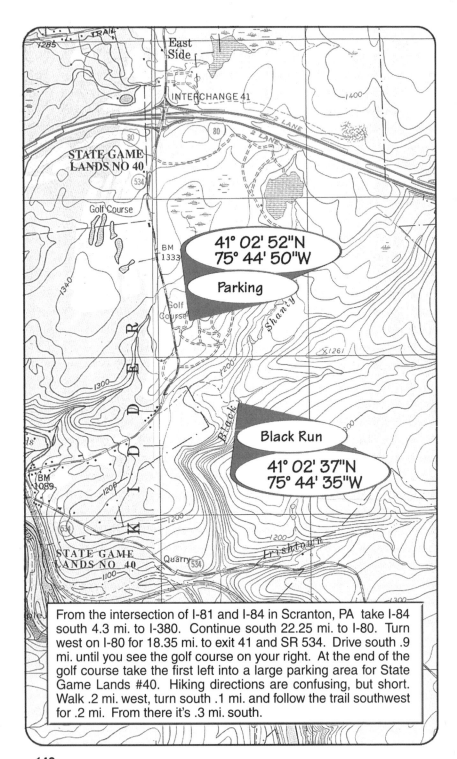

41° 02' 52"N
75° 44' 50"W

Parking

Black Run

41° 02' 37"N
75° 44' 35"W

From the intersection of I-81 and I-84 in Scranton, PA take I-84 south 4.3 mi. to I-380. Continue south 22.25 mi. to I-80. Turn west on I-80 for 18.35 mi. to exit 41 and SR 534. Drive south .9 mi. until you see the golf course on your right. At the end of the golf course take the first left into a large parking area for State Game Lands #40. Hiking directions are confusing, but short. Walk .2 mi. west, turn south .1 mi. and follow the trail southwest for .2 mi. From there it's .3 mi. south.

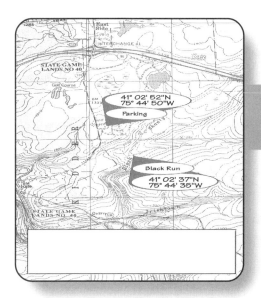

Black Run

Black Run travels due south and runs across about 120 yards of exposed rock. The stone causes several small cascades before concluding in a four foot drop that creates the swimming hole about 40 feet long and half as wide. It's bounded on the cascades west by a good ledge several feet above a small sweet spot that will be around seven feet deep. Take a deep breath when you jump in. Water is so cold in late September that the brook trout were wearing sweaters.

Getting to the hole is not physically difficult, but it is confusing. Access is though state game lands where the path is mowed in a crazy quilt pattern that provides and optimum combination of forage and protection for wildlife and maximum confusion for hikers. Once down at creek, follow a fisherman's trail south from the fire ring. Mild bushwhacking required.

I found some depressing litter at the fire ring, a case of Heineken. Typically it's bargain brands littering the outdoors. People with enough taste to drink good beer, generally have the sense to carry out the empties and not leave them around the campfire. On that topic, it should be pointed out that fires are illegal on game lands in Pennsylvania. So is swimming, though for a time it was legal to "bob and wade." The distinction seems even more silly than the law itself. Several states prohibit swimming to limit their liability, but it's rarely enforced.

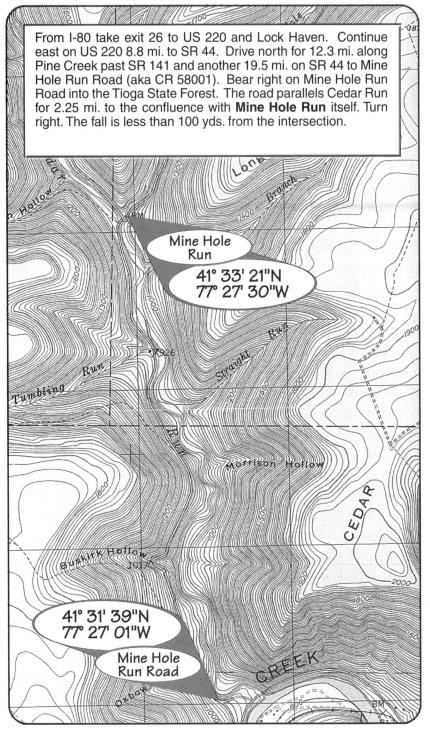

From I-80 take exit 26 to US 220 and Lock Haven. Continue east on US 220 8.8 mi. to SR 44. Drive north for 12.3 mi. along Pine Creek past SR 141 and another 19.5 mi. on SR 44 to Mine Hole Run Road (aka CR 58001). Bear right on Mine Hole Run Road into the Tioga State Forest. The road parallels Cedar Run for 2.25 mi. to the confluence with **Mine Hole Run** itself. Turn right. The fall is less than 100 yds. from the intersection.

Mine Hole
Run

41° 33' 21"N
77° 27' 30"W

41° 31' 39"N
77° 27' 01"W

Mine Hole
Run Road

Mine Hole

Mine Hole Run drains part of the plateau above Pennsylvania's Grand Canyon. It's a very small watershed, barely 10 square miles, with a steep gradient that drops more than 1,000 feet in just over 4.5 miles. At the very bottom of the run, water takes several leaps through a narrow cascades and bounces against a tall wall that helps form a modest swimming place. The wall is close to 30 feet high, considerably taller than the pool is wide. Any jumps? Not without your kneecaps becoming lodged in your larynx.

Despite the verticality, the pool is barely six feet deep. The rock structure isn't so great. There is virtually no impound at the bottom and the rock is so brittle that there's just an awful lot of freestone. The way it works out is that the velocity of the water shoves a few truck loads of cobble into the downstream end, making it deeper than a wading pool, but not deep enough to call a hole. Man, if you could just get in there with a backhoe.

The horizontal isn't that great, either. Just a couple of rocks to squat on. The main charm is the location, tucked just around the corner from a frequently traveled two-lane road. You dodge off on this side road and discover the dramatic rock. It's a nice surprise.

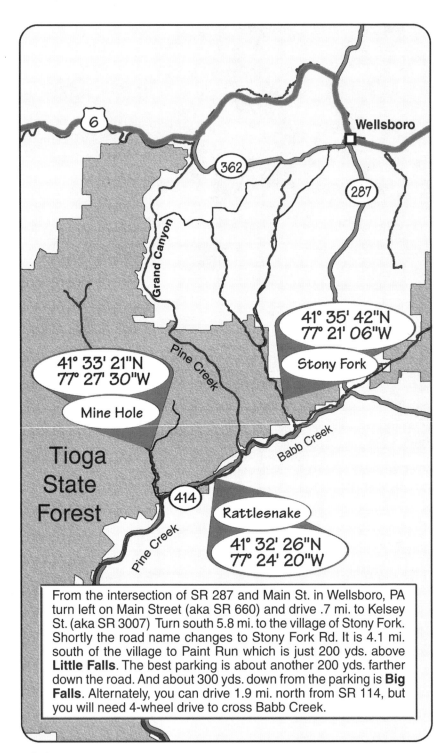

US 6

362

287 Wellsboro

Grand Canyon

41° 35' 42"N
77° 21' 06"W

Stony Fork

41° 33' 21"N
77° 27' 30"W

Pine Creek

Mine Hole

Babb Creek

Tioga
State
Forest

414

Rattlesnake

Pine Creek

41° 32' 26"N
77° 24' 20"W

From the intersection of SR 287 and Main St. in Wellsboro, PA
turn left on Main Street (aka SR 660) and drive .7 mi. to Kelsey
St. (aka SR 3007) Turn south 5.8 mi. to the village of Stony Fork.
Shortly the road name changes to Stony Fork Rd. It is 4.1 mi.
south of the village to Paint Run which is just 200 yds. above
Little Falls. The best parking is about another 200 yds. farther
down the road. And about 300 yds. down from the parking is **Big
Falls**. Alternately, you can drive 1.9 mi. north from SR 114, but
you will need 4-wheel drive to cross Babb Creek.

Rattlesnake Rock

Rattlesnake is distinguished by the rock, not the reptiles. It's a broad table of solid stone several feet above Pine Creek. Like a wedge, it sticks out into the creek and chisels off a lobe of water that cycles into broad pool big enough to do the backstroke. Actually, the pool is a little too large. The water at the back stagnates, but the swimming is fine right under the rock. Whether it's deep enough to jump from depends on water level.

Rattlesnake Rock is a large parking area at the southern end of the West Rim Trail. The trail is a well marked and maintained trail running 30-miles on a plateau high above Pine Creek through the portion known as Pennsylvania's Grand Canyon. The trail generally lies 800 feet above the wooded gorge and has been called the best trail in the state.

Even if you're not big into hiking, Rattlesnake is a good place to enjoy the outdoors. It's is right along State Route 414. Plus, there are flushing toilets!

From Lock Haven. PA take US 220 east to SR 44. Turn north for for 10.25 mi along Pine Creek to SR 414. Continue north along Pine Creek on SR 414 for 22.75 mi.es to the well marked parking area for Rattlesnake Rock.

Big Falls

Stony Fork

Totally impressive. At Big Falls water hits some very finely bedded, wafer-thin rock. It gouges out a short trough 20 feet long then drops into a pool that flares into a tasty container 60 feet long and 20 feet wide. A long, razor-straight, concrete-smooth slab of rock forms the entire eastern boundary of the pool. The action is on the far side, the western side. Really good jumping about the size of a horseshoe pit. Above that is a hemlock parkland with lots of picnicking. The lounging slabs are heavily shaded, but pool is open to the sky and there are fine views south, out of the canyon.

The water is the color of a wet chalk board. Depth was difficult to guess because the water is cloudy, but it does have two of the best engineered rope swings I've seen. There's a cable between two trees more than 30 feet above the water with a couple of lines hanging from it.

Upstream is Little Fall. The best hole is directly below the fall. Very good rock on the near side where there's an intact block that's nice and smooth on top about 12 feet off the surface of the water. I doubt it's jumpable. It doesn't seem the water gets much more than seven feet deep.

The place was extremely well picked up, but obviously heavily used. Water quality is suspect and some brown algae and seeps make footing slippery.

Watrous

Drive-up party spot.

Sand Run

Gorgeous fall. Ugly crowd.

Falling Spring

In the Pennsylvania Grand Canyon. A steep wall and a bend in Pine Creek 6.8 miles north of Blackwell, PA.

Naval Run

A fall .3 mi. from parking and a fair pool about .5 mi. farther. Locals complain about skinny dippers.

Angel Falls

A drip, a dribble, a drop, a flop.

Fallbrook Falls

A fall is all. No swimming hole.

Pirate Rock

High school party spot in the Tioga River.

Haystack

Loyalsock Creek. Human waste. Yuk!

Ricketts Glen

As many as 1,000 people on weekends. No swimming.

Potts Falls

Deep hole in Meshoppen Creek. Poor setting. Nasty water.

Little Rocky Glen

Tunkhannock Creek. Big billows of brown foam.

Seven Tubs

Luzerne County Park outside of Willkes-Barre. Overrun.

Hawk Falls

Shallow pools. Frequently visited.

Monongahela
Headwaters

From Uniontown, PN and the intersection os US 40 and US 119, continue east on US 40 for 15.5 mi. to Farmington and the intersection of SR 382. Turn left, downhill and into Ohiopyle State Park. The parking area is on the right just above Meadow Run's confluence with the Ohiopyle River.

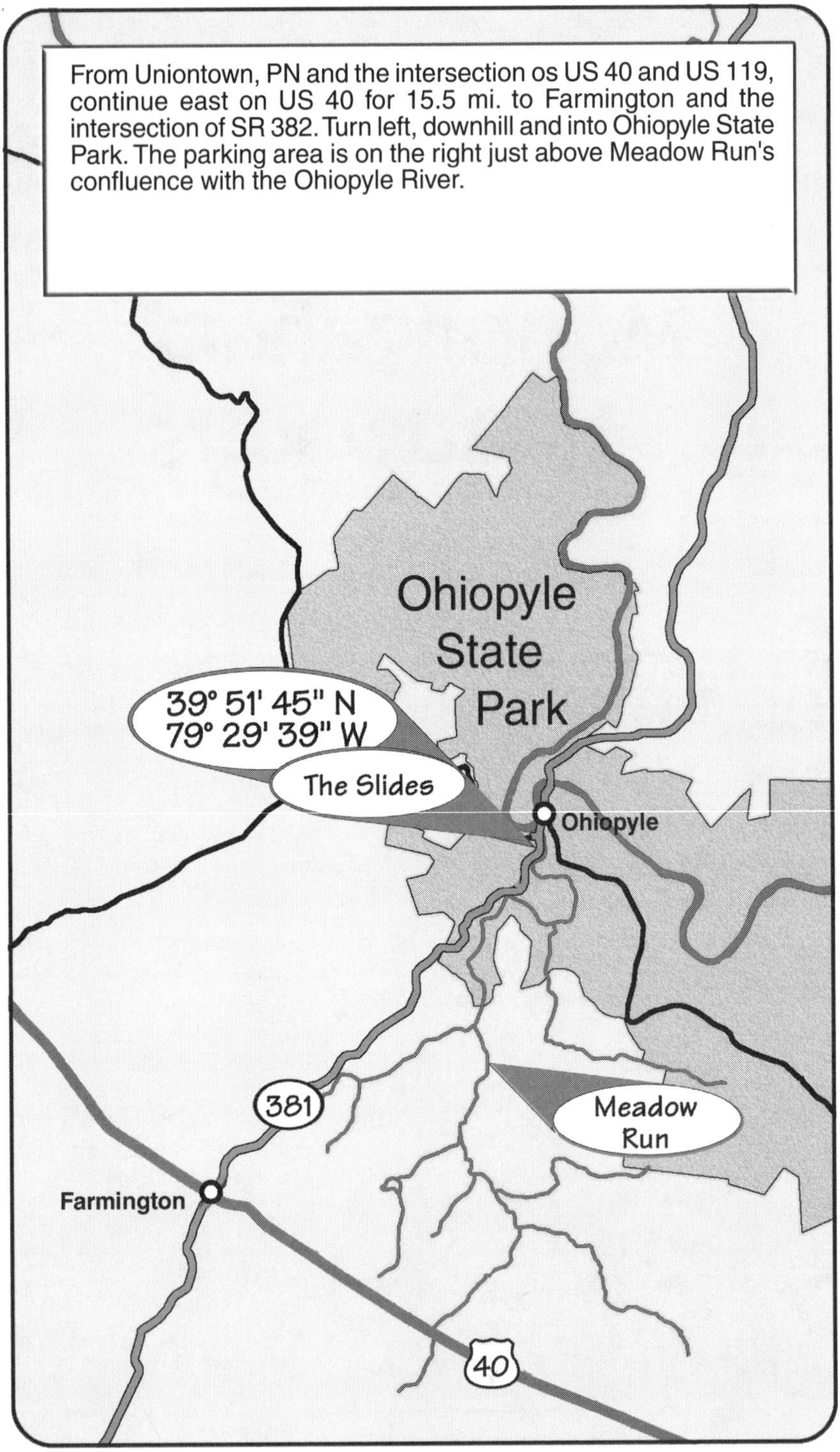

Ohiopyle
State
Park

39° 51' 45" N
79° 29' 39" W

The Slides

Ohiopyle

381

Meadow
Run

Farmington

40

Meadow Run

About 90 minutes southeast of Pittsburgh, Meadow Run is among the top five waterslides east of the Mississippi River. Depending on water level you can ride 100 feet and more. Just before its confluence with the Youghiogheny River at the town of Ohiopyle, Meadow Run carries visitors through a corkscrew flume of rock before delivering them – grinning broadly – into a modest pool below. Pamela Hall, an Ohiopyle native, says that during high water you can do the entire length of the slide.

"We spent hours there during the summer. We wore out more shorts; we'd have to take two pairs. And when we got home our mother used to bless us for ruining another pair." Hall recommends cutoffs. No bathing suits, no Speedos.

The Youghiogheny below Ohiopyle is one of the most popular white water destinations in the Northeast. When you get tired of the slide you can watch the paddlers or explore the river by foot, or bike along a converted railroad right of way.

Note: You will immediately identify yourself as an outsider if you try to pronounce the entire name of the Youghiogheny River. Paddlers and locals simply call it "The Yawk."

In Morgantown, WV, from exit 4 on I-68 take SR 7 south 9.6 mi. to Masontown and CR 23. Travel east on CR 23 for 1 mi. to CR 21 (aka Depot/Herring Rd.) Turn north on CR 21 (aka Bull Run Rd.) 2.4 mi. and bear right onto CR 14/4 (aka Mt Nebo/Bull Run Rd.) Descend a narrow, winding road 2 mi. to a sketchy bridge over the Cheat River. Cross to the eastern bank and drive less than 400 yds. to the first switchback. Look for the parking area on the left. Climb 100 yds., then start looking for steep descent on left that leads to **Blue Hole on Big Sandy Creek**.

39° 35' 48"N
79° 44' 41"W

Blue Hole

Blue Hole

It's law in West Virginia. A student at UWV in Morgantown may not earn a degree without spending at least one afternoon at Blue Hole. This portion of Big Sandy Creek has what must be the second best naturally occurring sand beach West Virginia. It's 800 square feet that slopes down into a big streak of deep water running right down the middle of a fat, fat hole. You could land a float plane in it.

It all happens where the creek hits a hunk of solid rock and doglegs to the right. The result is a hole about 80 yards long with a steep crescent-shaped beach on the inside turn. The rock faces generally east and measures about 100 feet long. It steps down in ledges to submerged shelves for about 35 linear feet to a dropoff. The middle portion is the jumping rock and is about 15 feet high. Most of the rest of the rock face suffers from submerged ledges that inhibit jumping unless you have bungees for quadriceps and can get the 20 feet of clearance required.

The swimming hole was clean when I saw it. Minor graffiti, but no trash. That's not always the case. The spur trail is plenty steep, but at about 50 yards, not nearly long enough to discourage the bozos and yahoos who, drink cheap beer and litter. Apart from the map on the opposite page, about the best way to find Blue Hole is to look for empties, mainly trash brands. If you find a case of Busch Lite empties, you're there.

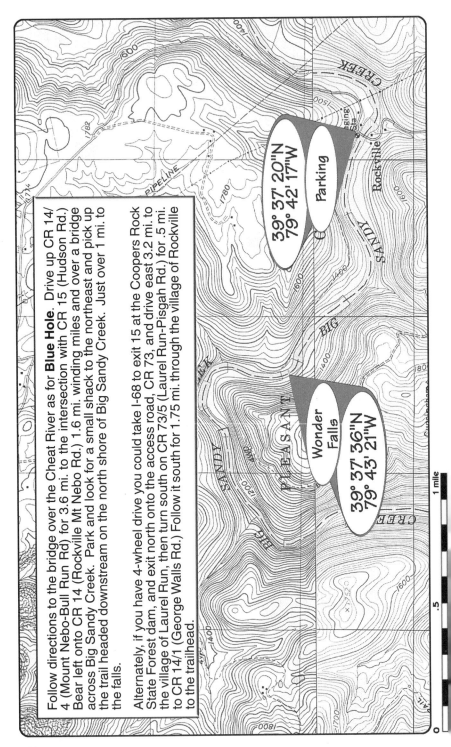

Follow directions to the bridge over the Cheat River as for **Blue Hole**. Drive up CR 14/4 (Mount Nebo-Bull Run Rd) to the intersection with CR 15 (Hudson Rd.) for 3.6 mi. Bear left onto CR 14 (Rockville Mt Nebo Rd.) 1.6 mi. winding miles and over a bridge across Big Sandy Creek. Park and look for a small shack to the northeast and pick up the trail headed downstream on the north shore of Big Sandy Creek. Just over 1 mi. to the falls.

Alternately, if you have 4-wheel drive you could take I-68 to exit 15 at the Coopers Rock State Forest dam, and exit north onto the access road, CR 73, and drive east 3.2 mi. to the village of Laurel Run, then turn south on CR 73/5 (Laurel Run-Pisgah Rd.) for .5 mi. to CR 14/1 (George Walls Rd.) Follow it south for 1.75 mi. through the village of Rockville to the trailhead.

39° 37' 20"N
79° 42' 17"W

Parking

Wonder
Falls

39° 37' 36"N
79° 43' 21"W

.5

1 mile

Wonder Fall

A magnificent cauldron close 70 feet across and twice as long. It's by the grace of the Pottsville group, sandstone mixed with thin beds of shale. When the Big Sandy Creek broke through the sandstone into the softer shale below, it eroded the underlying rock, which in turn caused the sandstone to collapse. In the not-too-distant geologic past sandstone ledges may have surrounded this hole by as much as 270 degrees. It must have been *absolutely* gorgeous. Now it's simply gorgeous.

The fall is around 18 feet high and a popular drop for paddlers in winter. During lower summer flows it's suitable for swimming. The above photo was taken at 3.8 feet on the Rockville gauge just upstream. Depth in the hole was hard to judge because water was dark and a little cloudy. Entry and exit is a problem. On the river right you need to do some climbing to get from the trail down to the water below the falls. Long legs are helpful. Better yet, hope that a ladder is placed to the left of the fall as it sometimes is.

No lounging below the fall, but huge amounts of solid, flat creek bed stretch 400 yards up from the fall. It's almost flat enough to drive upstream...and there are plenty who would like to. ATVs have hogged out the trail to such an extent that it was a *muddy mucking fess* when I visited during relative drought. Much of the area surrounding the fall is degraded and that the rating of an otherwise classic swimming hole.

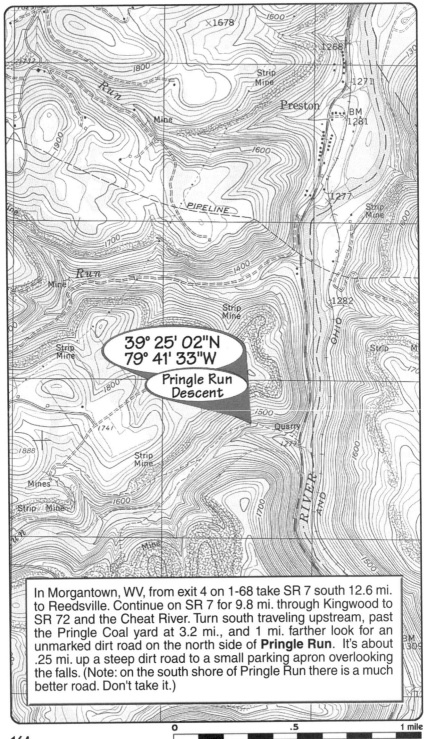

39° 25' 02"N
79° 41' 33"W

Pringle Run
Descent

In Morgantown, WV, from exit 4 on I-68 take SR 7 south 12.6 mi. to Reedsville. Continue on SR 7 for 9.8 mi. through Kingwood to SR 72 and the Cheat River. Turn south traveling upstream, past the Pringle Coal yard at 3.2 mi., and 1 mi. farther look for an unmarked dirt road on the north side of **Pringle Run**. It's about .25 mi. up a steep dirt road to a small parking apron overlooking the falls. (Note: on the south shore of Pringle Run there is a much better road. Don't take it.)

0   .5   1 mile

Pringle Run

It's a big, round hole cored straight into pale yellow rock and dressed with dense, dark green fringe of hemlock and rhododendron. A dandy fall just above the main fork of the Cheat River with 180 degrees of surrounding rock and unbelievable headward erosion that has left it undercut by as much as 10 feet at the lip. That's almost as deep as the fall is tall. So charmed is this place that even the rock that clutters the pool has the advantage of being nice flat slabs that make for excellent seating. The water color and clarity is superb, but for all the wrong reasons. The starling color is probably due to metals like aluminum that have leached into the stream from the mines above. And part of the rock's pale yellow tinge is also from the mines.

It's a really puzzling creek bed at low water, kind of like one of those fun houses where the floor is tilted. Above the fall, water runs 200 linear feet along a creek bed with many, many small tiers less than one foot high. You'd think the water would seek the lowest level. But because the creek bed is tilted a few degrees to the river left, the water sloshes in that direction and exits the fall lip at a point higher than the lowest point of the creek bed.

Visitorship is mainly local and the place was generally free of litter when I visited. Several superannuated washing machines and retired refrigerators dumped at the bottom of the road suggest that this might not always be the case.

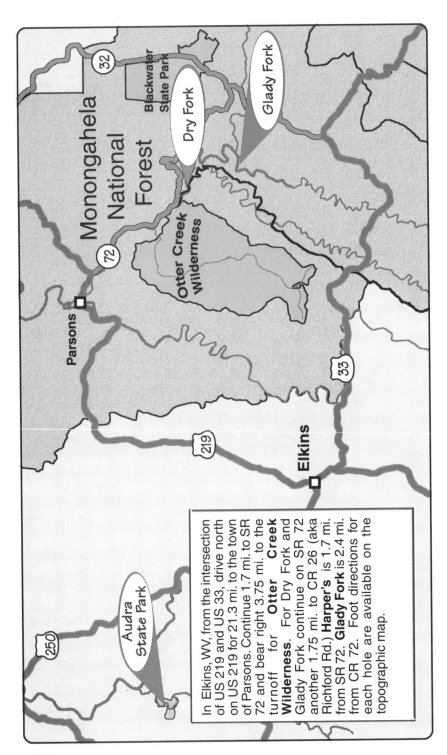

In Elkins, WV, from the intersection of US 219 and US 33, drive north on US 219 for 21.3 mi. to the town of Parsons. Continue 1.7 mi. to SR 72 and bear right 3.75 mi. to the turnoff for **Otter Creek Wilderness.** For Dry Fork and Glady Fork continue on SR 72 another 1.75 mi. to CR 26 (aka Richford Rd.) **Harper's** is 1.7 mi. from SR 72. **Glady Fork** is 2.4 mi. from CR 72. Foot directions for each hole are available on the topographic map.

Monongahela
National
Forest

Otter Creek
Wilderness

Blackwater
State Park

Dry Fork

Glady Fork

Parsons

Elkins

Audra
State Park

32

72

33

219

250

Glady Fork

The Cheat River has more forks than the Queen of England's silver drawer. The Dry Fork, the Laurel Fork, Shavers Fork, Black Fork...Here is one more, the Glady Fork. Whereas the upper part of the Laurel Fork is wild and remote, the lower part of the Glady Fork is the place to look for solitude, thanks in part to road washouts and trail collapses.

There is a pretty good swimming hole at the first wash. It's about thirty feet long and six feet deep. There's a riffle at the top of the pool then the river flares wide and the water slows enough to make this a good spot for moderate levels. The photo above was taken with the gauge at Evenwood measured 68. Velocity was around one foot per second, which is to say manageable for someone who can swim. Check the web site for a link to live gauge levels.

Some hard rock cleaves off nice and flat, making good forms for an afternoon spent listening to water traveling all the way from Pocahontas County at the top of the Monongahela National Forest. Privacy lifts rating from fair to good.

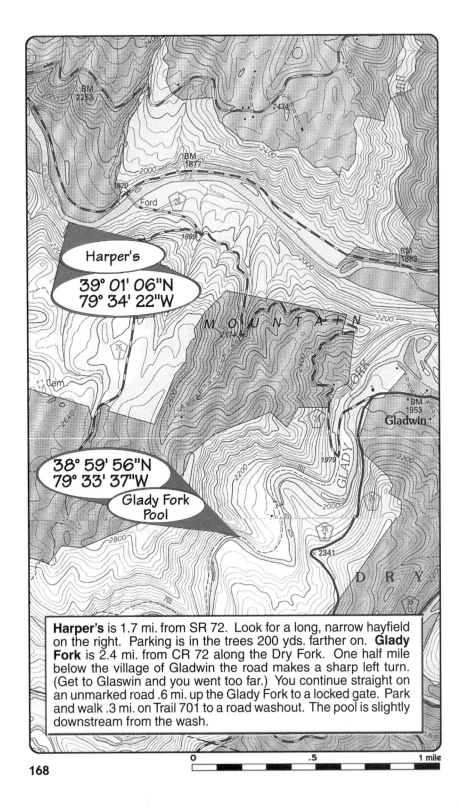

Harper's

39° 01' 06"N
79° 34' 22"W

38° 59' 56"N
79° 33' 37"W

Glady Fork
Pool

Harper's is 1.7 mi. from SR 72. Look for a long, narrow hayfield on the right. Parking is in the trees 200 yds. farther on. **Glady Fork** is 2.4 mi. from CR 72 along the Dry Fork. One half mile below the village of Gladwin the road makes a sharp left turn. (Get to Glaswin and you went too far.) You continue straight on an unmarked road .6 mi. up the Glady Fork to a locked gate. Park and walk .3 mi. on Trail 701 to a road washout. The pool is slightly downstream from the wash.

0   .5   1 mile

Dry Fork

It's the sort of place schoolboys go when they're skipping class or where good ol' boys go when they call in sick. You can swim laps onthis fork of the Cheat River. It's a good 75 feet long and 20 feet wide. Out in the middle of the channel the depth is about eight feet. The beach is marginal, an enormous gravel bar on river right containing the crunched up bones of Rich Mountain. It slopes down into the river opposite some low ledges on river left. They contain some decent slabs for sitting on and it looks like you can achieve some simple dives. One spot looks like it's around eight feet off the water. Lots of open sky and good sun.

It's a community type swimming hole, mainly just a drive up. It's not public land, but neither was it posted when I visited. Nevertheless, locals said other owners have closed some swimming holes along the road because they were sick of picking up other people's trash.

To find it follow the map on the left. Look on the right for a path that leads through a grassy field to the river. Parking is 200 yards farther on in some trees. To check water levels go to our web site for a link to the gauge at Gladwin.

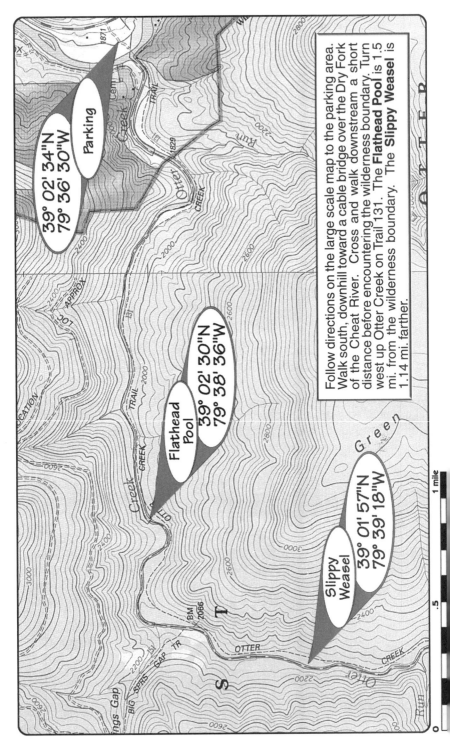

39° 02' 34"N
79° 36' 30"W

Parking

39° 02' 30"N
79° 38' 36"W

Flathead
Pool

39° 01' 57"N
79° 39' 18"W

Slippy
Weasel

Follow directions on the large scale map to the parking area. Walk south, downhill toward a cable bridge over the Dry Fork of the Cheat River. Cross and walk downstream a short distance before encountering the wilderness boundary. Turn west up Otter Creek on Trail 131. The **Flathead Pool** is 1.5 mi. from the wilderness boundary. The **Slippy Weasel** is 1.14 mi. farther.

Flathead Pool

A good low water, warm weather spot. Typical water temp in this part of the Monongahela National Forest goes from pretty darn cold to really damn cold. The pool is formed by a couple of large boulders in the Otter Creek Wilderness. They pinch Otter Creek together and give the water enough velocity to keep the cobble cleared out. Dimension is roughly 50 feet long, 20 to 30 feet wide and seven feet deep in the middle. The canopy is almost complete with hemlock on the trail side of the creek and beech and maple on the far side that practically grow together over the creek.

Another interesting factor is the wall on the right as you look upstream. A low wall of what's probably limestone has some really interesting erosion on it, tiny potholes so close together — separated in some places by inches. It looks like the crater pocked surface of the moon.

This hole is barely visible from the trail. You can see a big rock, the corner of which pops up above the level of the trail. The best way to locate the pool is to look for a poplar tree about 20 inches in diameter that has fallen over the trail just high enough for hiker to walk under it.

The gauge at Evenwood was 47 when the above photos were taken.

High Falls

Slippy Weasel

A typical boulder hole. Two medium size boulders squeeze Otter Creek together such that it's about three feet across, but very hydraulic. The pool below is about thirty feet long and half as wide. Depth in the pool was seven to eight feet when the Evenwood gauge was at 47. You'll find one really good sunning rock opposite the trail and a deeply shaded rock trail side. The sunning rock faces south so you'll get good rays, but it's immediately trail side. Not lots of privacy, so better keep your trunks on. Fifty yards above you find a longer, more relaxed pool. It's got a cascade at the top and lots of rock at the hem. Seating there is lousy.

A little less than one mile up is a ford with a fabulous sand beach. No swimming hole, though. About one hundred yards after the ford start looking left for a descending trail that leads to a nice little fall with a flat bench of land above it.

The trail continues generally south. One mile above is a small, aggressive fall seven to eight feet tall. Very muscular and with lots of rock clutter, but the fan-shaped pool at the bottom may be usable at lower levels. Farther still, at Morris Run, you'll find a smooth, limestone vastness. Although the main channel is well directed and quite tight, it's not strong enough to blow out a hole. The deepest it gets is four feet. On the whole, a great place to lie on the rocks and take it easy when you're visiting the Monongahela National Forest, but that's all.

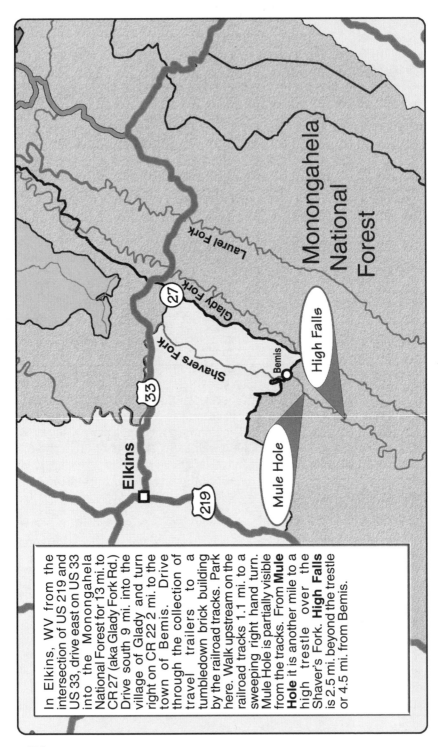

In Elkins, WV from the intersection of US 219 and US 33, drive east on US 33 into the Monongahela National Forest for 13 mi. to CR 27 (aka Glady Fork Rd.) Drive south 9 mi. into the village of Glady and turn right on CR 22 2 mi. to the town of Bemis. Drive through the collection of travel trailers to a tumbledown brick building by the railroad tracks. Park here. Walk upstream on the railroad tracks 1.1 mi. to a sweeping right hand turn. Mule Hole is partially visible from the tracks. From **Mule Hole** it is another mile to a high trestle over the Shaver's Fork. **High Falls** is 2.5 mi. beyond the trestle or 4.5 mi. from Bemis.

Monongahela National Forest

Laurel Fork

Glady Fork

Shavers Fork

27

33

219

Elkins

Bemis

High Falls

Mule Hole

High Falls

Fast water meets soft rock with excellent effect here on the Shavers Fork of the Cheat River. It's four or five times wider than the average width of the river and it has an arc of at least 120 degrees. Very impressive. The cause is likely shale from the New River formation resting under harder sandstone. The river works its way into the softer rock and erodes it faster than the sandstone above — similar to the process at Wonder Fall. With the support of the underlying rock gone, the sandstone collapses.

The fall is eight to ten feet high and the water is deep enough for jumping. There's virtually no place to sit below the fall on the near side. Just a cobble beach. Plenty of good seating on the opposite shore where the soft rock is so deeply undercut that a roof extends 10 feet over a ledge. Also, when water is low there's plenty of room to kick back above on the smooth, flat sandstone.

A stair leads down to the river from some train tracks that are maintained for rail excursions. The former Maryland Western and abandoned railroads like it have been taken over by tour operators providing rail junkets throughout the Monongahela National Forest. For info about train departure times and fares, contact 877-686-7245 or visit www.mountainrail.com For hiking directions, see the map at left.

BIRTHPLACE OF RIVERS

Here mountain waters divide into many rivers. Greenbrier, Gauley and Elk start south and west to the Kanawha; the Jackson east to the James; north goes the South Branch to the Potomac, and the Cheat and Tygart to the Monongahela.

WEST VIRGINIA DEPARTMENT OF ARCHIVES AND HISTORY 1970

Pocahontas County

Mule Hole

An underwater canyon. The Shavers Fork of the Cheat River meets a geologic boundary of softer stone where it has undercut the bed rock to such a degree that almost one third of the swimming hole's total volume is under a stone roof. It's not at all apparent to an observer unless the water level is extremely low. (Above photo taken with the Bemis gauge at 3 feet.) I visited a couple of times before I figured it out. It seems like you're standing on a smooth block of rock right at the water's edge when in fact you're standing on rim of stone that extends as far as ten feet out over the water.

"You put a mask on and dive down in there and it's like a cave," said Rob Mullennex, who's been visiting Mule Hole for 25 years. "It's as deep as 13 feet. When the water is lower you can stand up on a ledge behind the fall and count the pebbles in the bottom. That's how clear the water is."

It's a well-loved place that, because of its low relief, is favored for camping. It's just far enough from the parking area that campers who like luxury need to be industrious about getting their kit and caboodle to the swimming hole. Mullennex and his half dozen friends used a wheelbarrow to transport an estimated 1,200 pounds of gear, food and beverages for their annual campout. An earlier group of college students visiting the Monongahela National Forest reportedly fashioned a dolly to fit the railroad tracks in order to transpor beer kegs just over one mile from Bemis.

Quarry Run

39° 39' 28"N
79° 50' 31"W

Actually an inlet on Cheat Lake. Not that remarkable.

Audra State Park

39° 02' 31"N
80° 04' 02"W

At least one dozen places along the Middle Fork River where it passes through the park. Not lots of vertical but plenty of horizontal. Surprisingly deep given it's width. Really pretty slate color. Major family spot.

Whitaker Falls

38° 31' 30"N
80° 11' 01"W

One broad basin by a county road (CR 49, Valley Fork Rd.). Fascinating rock, though. A bank to bank bed of solid rock 100 yards long or more. Low angle though and consequently, no pool and not even steep enough for a slide, I doubt. Still, I bet it's impressive during higher flows.

Faulkner

38° 54' 44"N
79° 43' 17"W

A popular spot in the Shavers Fork of the Cheat River just below the fish hatchery. Lots of traffic from a huge collection of summer vacation trailers in the community of Faulkner.

Stuart Park

38° 55' 20"N
79° 46' 42"W

Shavers Fork of the Cheat River in the Monongahela National Forest. A day use area that's undistinguished compared to other places in the chapter.

Gauley, Cranberry & Williams River

From Fayetteville, WV at the intersection of SR 16 and US 19, drive north on US 19 for 20.25 mi. and take the last left before the Gauley Bridge over the Summersville Lake onto **Whippoorwill** Rd. Follow this short, road curving right past two spur roads to a third road that goes less than 100 yds. into woods before it's blocked off. A trail leading left goes down to the water. The trail to the right goes to the top of a rock wall.

Campsites

Campsite

Whippoorwill

38° 12' 40"N
80° 52' 06"W

L A K E

ELE

1800

1800

1800

1800

LANDING ST

Point

Long

GAULEY

SUMMERSVILLE

1800

1962

19

41

JEEP

38° 14' 01"N
80° 51' 18"W

Long Point

1800

RIVER

BM
1922

For **Long Point**, you have to get a boat and motor to it. There's a way to walk around to the top, but I'm not going to publish it 'cause the jump is so potentially dangerous that it's safer to take watercraft and climb as high as skill and conditioning permit, then let loose.

0   .5   1 mile

Whippoorwill

Another high adventure spot on Summersville Lake in the Gauley River National Recreation Area. 'The Whip" is a sheer, west-facing wall that rises about 80 feet off the lake level. It's a popular climbing spot, due in part to the setting and also because the rock is mainly sheer. It's got great adhesion for climbing since the rock is so fresh, only recently exposed when a chunk cracked loose leaving an impressive roof at about 60 feet off the water. Anchors at the top mean you can lower to a ledge about 40 feet off the surface.

Alicia Landis, a climbing goddess, has a tiny scar on her chin that she earned at The Whip just after uttering what are statistically the four most dangerous words in the English language, "Hey guys, watch this."

"If you're climbing and want to turn it into a dive, get a good push off," she says fingering the knick in her mandible.

The nice thing about The Whip is that you don't need to use a boat to get there and, unlike most other places on the lake, it's not so convenient for motorized watercraft to visit. So there is some peace. Open sky to the west and south means that it gets toasty warm. There is a place about the form of a king-sized bed six feet above the anchor. Not a lot of comfortable shade, though. All the cover is low and brushy.

Long Point

Long Point

Sick and twisted cliff jumping. Depending on the level at Summersville Lake, the ride can be as much as 100 vertical feet into water deep enough to stop a load of bricks. One regular said that she wears a ski vest to soften the impact and to keep her afloat if she gets knocked out.

The only practical access is from the water and you need to have solid climbing skills. Consider that you'll have to climb with wet tips and toes, plus you have to be a stud to make the overhanging corner to the best release spots. Robert Thomas (pictured top, left) qualifies.

"The overhanging corner is the best release spot," he says. "If you lose it, you won't have to push off at the last second. Once you're on that corner you can climb 'til you start getting shaky and then just let go."

There doesn't appear to be a nontechnical way to the top from water level. Rather, you have to drive to the airport, park and hike into the Gauley River National Recreation Area for about two miles to the point, then have a boat waiting to pick you up after you jump. I didn't see any bolts at the top that'd allow you to run a rope down to water level. Any natural anchors were several yards back from the vertical face. If you're still tempted to go from the top, be advised this can be a fatal plunge

For **Lower Meadow River** start from the intersection of SR 16 and US 19 in Fayetteville, WV. Drive north across the New River Gorge 6.9 mi. to US 60. Exit north and drive 400 yds. to CR 4 (Sunday Rd.) and turn right toward the Gauley River National Recreation Area. Follow Sunday Rd. 3.5 mi. to CR 60/10 (Miller Ridge Rd.) Take Miller Ridge south .3 mi. to the village of Clifty and CR 4/4 (Shawvers Bridge) Turn left .8 mi. to small parking area. Park carefully as not to block farm roads or gates. See topo for hiking details.

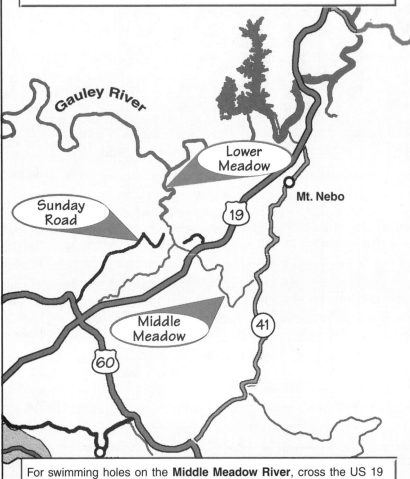

Gauley River

Lower Meadow

Mt. Nebo

Sunday Road

19

Middle Meadow

41

60

For swimming holes on the **Middle Meadow River**, cross the US 19 bridge over the Meadow River. Continue another .6 mi. to CR 24/9 (Underwood Rd.) Turn left, then make an immediate left on a dirt road. Drive .25 mi. to an informal parking area and start looking for an ATV trail descending to the river. See topo maps for additional info on hiking

Pro Tour

From the parking area described on the preceding map, look for an ATV trail descending northeast for .5 mi. and 250 vertical feet to an abandoned rail grade, then turn left, downstream. For **Coming Home** walk approximately 1,000 feet and start looking for a barely discernible trail descending to the river. There might be a rock about the size of a boombox stacked on top of another rock to mark the trail. **Gateway** is about 600 yds. downstream from where you first encounter the rail grade.

Coming Home

A true day-long swimming hole. It has a mondo sunning rock big enough for you and all your friends. Nice and flat on a slackwater pool on the Meadow River with low-angle dives in all directions. You have to swim to get there, but over on the eastern side you get the good afternoon sunshine. If you arrive earlier in the day, you can get sun at a small sand pocket on the near side. No high vertical. Settlement higher on the river means that the water quality is only good.

It can be difficult to find. When you get to the rail grade there is a berm that separates the trail from the creek. Shortly after the berm flattens out, start looking for a barely discernible trail descending to the river. There might be a rock about the size of a boombox stacked on top of another rock to mark the trail.

Suitable for mountain bikes, also. There are a couple of steep bends on the descending road that amount to a fun few hundred yards of advanced mountain bike trail. After that you're in the Gauley River National Recreation Area on a rail grade which is smooth and flat enough to play marbles.

Pictures were taken at very low water, 3.45 feet on the Mt. Lookout gauge or just over 100 cfs.

Gateway

The pools occur at the bottom of a rock garden. On the near side is a nice glob of rock that stands at the top of a great big hole. The rock is about six feet above the water and with plenty of room for a small group. Be forewarned that the Lower Meadow River is perhaps the most dangerous stretch of whitewater in the state. When it's pumping you can hear the deep grating sound of huge boulders being shoved downstream. Undercuts produce so many powerful holes that one paddler says, "you might be looking back at one of your buddies, then turn around seconds later and he's gone. Just disappeared underwater."

Of course those are not swimming conditions. Guides say that optimal paddling on the Lower Meadow is about 750 cfs. Locals say swimming shouldn't be considered at anything above 400 cfs. In my opinion it's even lower. Wait until the Mt. Lookout gauge is below 300 cfs or approximately 4.4 feet. Alternately, you can judge safety the low-tech way. Break a branch off a tree and toss it into the hole. If it washes out the bottom before you can get your clothes oft, you should think twice about getting in.

Bonus Feature: If you're on a bike and want some more exercise, pedal to the confluence with the Gauley River. There's a *huge* sand beach. But it's a party spot for ATVs.. Not worth a stay, but perhaps a visit. On the way there you pass through a long tunnel. At one point it's entirely dark, you can't see the light on either end. Spooky.

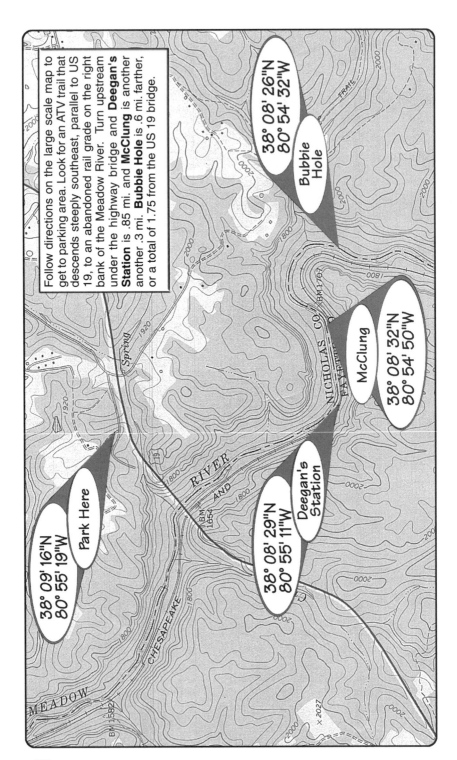

Follow directions on the large scale map to get to parking area. Look for an ATV trail that descends steeply southeast, parallel to US 19, to an abandoned rail grade on the right bank of the Meadow River. Turn upstream under the highway bridge and **Deegan's Station** is .85 mi. and **McClung** is another another .3 mi. **Bubbie Hole** is .6 mi. farther, or a total of 1.75 from the US 19 bridge.

38° 08' 26"N
80° 54' 32"W

Bubbie Hole

38° 08' 32"N
80° 54' 50"W

McClung

38° 08' 29"N
80° 55' 11"W

Deegan's Station

38° 09' 16"N
80° 55' 19"W

Park Here

Deegan's Station

A champion. Big enough to float a battleship and deep through-out. It's 180 feet on the major axis and 80 feet across. It happens where the river travels east to west through a rapid, then runs up on a highly eroded slab tilted against the Meadow River at a 35–degree angle. From there the river turns northeast and immediately flares into the main hole. Downstream towards the bottom of the hole is a nice sloping rock that you can sit on while dangling your feet in the water. Easy to jump off the nose of it. Bring sandals with sticky rubber because the steep angle makes the rocks difficult to remount for subsequent jumps.

Back at the top, there is a rope swing on the near side. You have to get some good clearance to make it into the sweet spot, but there is no really good launch. There is one spot to leap off, but there are substantial rocks in front. You best be able to tuck your knees up under your chin, or you're apt to have your toenails torn off.

Shade and seating: the top part of the hole is shaded with mixed forest, especially hemlock. The sand bar has lots of growth that detracts from seating. Best makes it over to the slab at the top of the hole. It has a king-size declivity that makes a perfect three-person lounge chair. Faces west, also. Killer afternoon spot if you're visiting the Gauley River National Recreation Area.

McClung

McClung

Just a big, big slackwater pool. A limestone ledge on the opposite side sort of mirrors the shape of the sand bar, more of which later. It's a very flat swimming hole. Nothing you can jump from. The best use is probably bobbing up and down with your beverage of choice. 'Nother great sand beach — 300 feet curving around the Meadow River. Trees are evenly spaced and that helps for shade and probably contributes to the deposition of sand. All this sand might be due in part to the strip mining that was carried on above. At any rate, the mines were closed long ago.

Moderate visitation and, thankfully, conspicuously clean when I reviewed it. Even unopened canned goods left behind from an earlier campout had been neatly stacked on a vinyl covered bench. If you're lucky to experience it by yourself as I did, it's a treasure.

Start looking for this hole about 20 minutes into the hike. The tip off is a corrugated steel shelter big enough for a couple automobiles. The hole is right beyond that.

Bubbie Hole

Bubbie Hole

A magnificently large rock the size of a small home splits the Meadow River and forces a bend in it. On the near side the river has banked up a pile of sand that's probably 15 feet deep. It slopes smack into the fat part of the pool and at such an angle that you can sprint downhill, kicking up sand as you pull off your shirt, fling it behind you and dive into the water. There is an equally good, perhaps better, pool on the other side of the rock. It's got a rope swing, but doesn't have any seating.

The rock island is 15 feet high at its tallest, that's at the upstream edge. It's only six to eight feet on the near side, however the lack of depth of the water between this rock and the beach may make jumping a little risky at lower levels like those pictured above.

The hole clearly gets use from foot traffic and perhaps ATVs. Not a scrap of litter though. Could mean people are exceptional citizens or that volunteers cleaned up right before I visited and that there are normally many beer cans and bait containers.

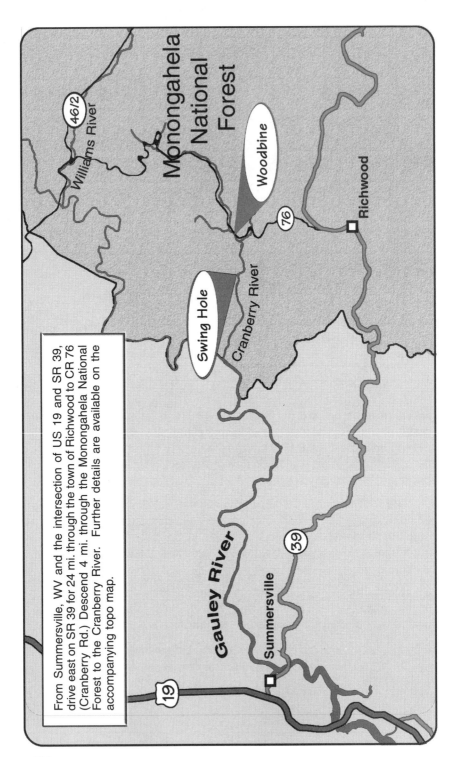

From Summersville, WV and the intersection of US 19 and SR 39, drive east on SR 39 for 24 mi. through the town of Richwood to CR 76 (Cranberry Rd.) Descend 4 mi. through the Monongahela National Forest to the Cranberry River. Further details are available on the accompanying topo map.

Monongahela National Forest

Williams River

46/2

Woodbine

76

Richwood

Swing Hole

Cranberry River

Gauley River

39

Summersville

19

Swing Hole

A couple of swimming holes, one better during higher levels, the other during lower water. Early in the season when water is higher, go a little over 400 yards upstream from Camp Splinter to the remnants of a cable crossing. The Cranberry River is a little deeper here due to some upstream boulders that apparently catch a lot of free stone that might otherwise occlude the bottom. Some people call it Swing Hole. However, the concrete footing and the steel poles that formed the anchors for the bridge are badly bent and barely high enough for a rope swing.

During low water conditions in the Monongahela National Forest, head downstream from Camp Splinter to a point about 50 yards below the portion of the river that's marked as catch and release. There's a basin about 30 feet long and when the sun hits the pale bottom just right, the color is beautiful. You'll likely have a couple of small, steep sand beaches to sit on. The sweet spot is about 12 feet by eight feet and it's overhead deep. Visit during higher water levels and it will of course be deeper, but there's not going to be anyplace to sit.

38° 17' 30"N
80° 32' 10"W

Woodbine

38° 17' 17"N
80° 33' 01"W

Swing Hole

For **Swing Hole** drive 2.25 mi. down Cranberry Rd. from SR 39 and turn left onto CR 7/2. At .75 mi. turn right on CR 7/5 (FS 83) and drive .4 mi. to a sharp left and descend 3.1 mi. to parking across a stream from Camp Splinter. Ford and walk upstream on the south bank of the Cranberry River for .3 mi. to Swing Hole. For **Woodbine** do not turn off Cranberry Road, but follow it 4 mi. from SR 39 to the Cranberry River. Turn left into the Woodbine Picnic Area and park in the first area.

Woodbine

If you don't think you can convince your kids to hike four miles into a wilderness spot in the Monongahela National Forest, you don't want to carry him and you don't mind crowds, then welcome to the Woodbine picnic area. The Cranberry River has a bedrock bottom here and long, low limestone ledges that produce a good channel of water that's highly accessible. A rock outcrop below and a collection of about one-half dozen boulders slow the water and make it deep enough for a rope swing.

Locals advise that if you try to swing straight out perpendicular to the river, you'll be out over a blind ledge when you let go. Rather, wrap the rope over the tree from the downstream side of the river. That makes the rope swing in an arc instead of a pendulum and puts you out into deeper water. This info courtesy of Nicole Anderson of Richwood. That's her older sister Miranda pictured above demonstrating more technique on water entry.

Three Forks of Williams River

Beechy Run

38° 19' 40"N
80° 19' 57"W

Middle Fork Trailhead

38° 20' 12"N
80° 22' 26"W

CRANBERRY WILDERNESS

From Summersville, WV and the intersection of US 19 and SR 41, take SR 41 east 12 mi. to Craigsville. Turn on SR 20 for 11 mi. through the town of Cowen to CR 46 (Williams River Rd.) Take the Williams River Rd. 12.25 mi. to a hard right turn onto FS 108 that leads .5 mi to the trailhead for the Cranberry Wilderness. It's 2.4 mi. up TR 271 to the confluence of **Beechy Run** and the Middle Fork Williams River. The tub is on Beechy just above the confluence.

Beechy Run

A modest feature in the Monongahela National Forest, but it gains points for being wilderness. Water is so clear that you can count the whiskers on a crayfish walking across the bottom of the creek. It's a low fall across a ledge 30 feet wide. A couple of large rocks offset from one another form a constriction that makes water flow fast enough to prevent the pool from filling entirely with sand and cobble. At about 20 feet across, the pool is big enough for a couple of strokes, but that's not its best use, according to Tom Easton, a DC area carpenter and back pain sufferer.

He said that walking up the trail to Big Beechy helped relieve pain and release some fluid from two discs that he herniated on the job. But if the Cranberry Wilderness seems a long way to go for occupational therapy, listen to this:

"In January and February the level is really up," Easton says. "There's a special seat off to the left as you look at the falls. Sitting in the fall with the cold water pounding on my back really reduces swelling."

He says that after a couple of treatments, he felt so much better that he fed his Vicodin and Flexeril to the chipmunks...not really, but I can report that the ground squirrels at the campsite adjoining the fall did seem unusually relaxed in his company.

South Fork Cherry River

A couple of hip-deep holes called **Chestnut** and **Willow**.

Pillow Rock

38° 12' 25"N
80° 56' 08"W

A steep trail from Carnifex State Park. Not really worth it as a swimming spot.

40-Foot

38° 08' 04"N
80° 52' 59"W

Gorgeous place right by State Route 41, part of the "Miracle Mile" on the Meadow River. I've seen more litter, but I can't remember when.

Rudolph Fall

38° 14' 20"N
80° 31' 45"W

A community swimming hole in town of Richwood, WV.

Big Rock

37° 17' 42"N
80° 31' 21"W

Marginal place upstream from Woodbine on the Cranberry River. Lots of campers.

Breedon Hole

In the Cherry River between LaFrank and Fenwick. Local swimming hole in settled area among houses. Also, **The Cut**, just above the confluence with Laurel Creek. Below the confluence, ignore **Matinee** behind the drive-in theater, **Road Garage** opposite the village of Curtin and the and bridge at the confluence with the Gauley River. All of it's highway and coal sidings.

Blue Ridge Highlands & the New River Gorge

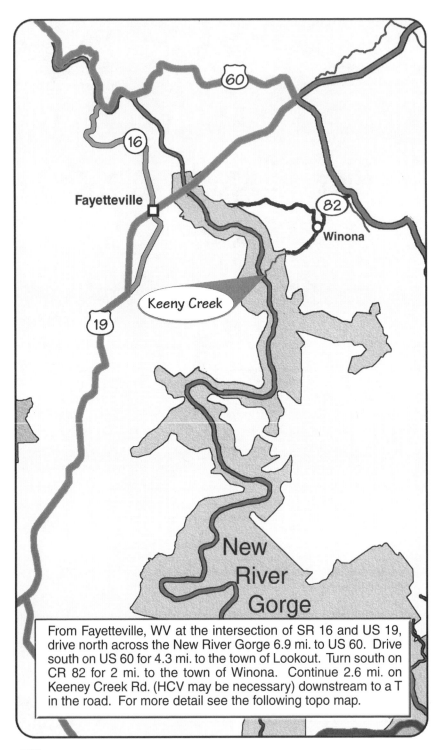

From Fayetteville, WV at the intersection of SR 16 and US 19, drive north across the New River Gorge 6.9 mi. to US 60. Drive south on US 60 for 4.3 mi. to the town of Lookout. Turn south on CR 82 for 2 mi. to the town of Winona. Continue 2.6 mi. on Keeney Creek Rd. (HCV may be necessary) downstream to a T in the road. For more detail see the following topo map.

Halls of Karma

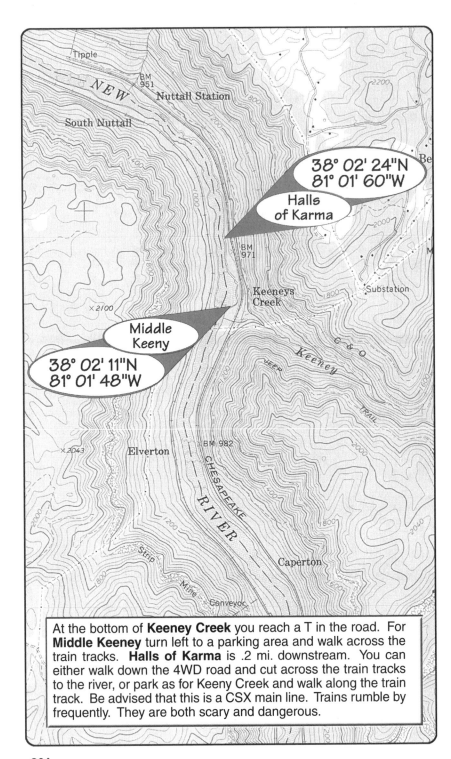

**38° 02' 24"N
81° 01' 60"W**

Halls
of Karma

Middle
Keeny

**38° 02' 11"N
81° 01' 48"W**

At the bottom of **Keeney Creek** you reach a T in the road. For **Middle Keeney** turn left to a parking area and walk across the train tracks. **Halls of Karma** is .2 mi. downstream. You can either walk down the 4WD road and cut across the train tracks to the river, or park as for Keeny Creek and walk along the train track. Be advised that this is a CSX main line. Trains rumble by frequently. They are both scary and dangerous.

Halls of Karma

Less than four miles upstream from the bridge over the New River Gorge, Halls of Karma is a magnificent rock terrace—almost an auditorium. There are literally hundreds of square feet to take in the sun and picnic. In addition to the terrace, a finger of rock extends toward the center of the water and creates a polite eddy 35 to 45 feet long in what is otherwise a huge, muscular white water river.

There's a set of stairs that step down into the water, but straight forward entry doesn't necessarily mean simple exit. It might be easy to find yourself too far out of the eddy, get swept downstream and turned into fish food. The park service discourages swimming. If you're not a bozo or yahoo, you can, in my opinion, cautiously enjoy this place at flow levels below 4,500 cfs which is when the accompanying picture was taken.

Best advice: Use Halls of Karma mainly for above-the-water recreation. Apart from potentially swift current, the New River can be yucky. It drains such a large area that funk abounds. So pack a picnic basket and bring some cocoa butter for your honey to rub on your while watching the paddlers go by. Better make sure the coconuts come from a tree with high SPF. The rock faces west and gets plenty of sun, even 1,000 feet down in the canyon.

Middle Keeny

Middle Keeney

The best beach in this book. Any water that runs with the velocity of the New River is going to grind up some rock. And where to put all that sand? Right at the bottom of Keeeny Rapids. So deep are the deposits that scarcely a rock pokes above its pale, powdery surface. It seems that deposition is caused by the morphology of the riverbed. Below the rapids the river flares momentarily and the bottom gets deeper. So when all the ground-up product of that tumbling bedload gets to this spot, it slows and settles out of suspension, especially on the river right in the slackwater pool that comprises the swimming hole. Result: a big open beach with enough room to put up a circus tent.

It's highly accessible. On the day I surveyed it I saw an old arthritic man bent over his walking stick and a twenty-something couple with their infant child. Same swimming caveat for this place as for Karma. The best part is above water. You can paddle around in the pool, but just a little too far out into the main channel and you're going to get your name in the newspaper.

From the parking area cross the railroad tracks just north of the bridge over Keeney Creek. Look for an obvious trail and walk less than 500 feet to the New River. You may be able to take an HCV down to the rapids, but road improvement was stalled for environmental reasons. Better plan on taking a 4-wheel drive.

From Beckley, WV at the intersection of I-64 and US 19 take I-64 east 4.9 mi. to exit 129 and Grandview Rd. South on CR 9 (aka Grandview Rd.) toward Shady Spring. Drive .6 mi. through a couple of hard left turns and immediately before a hard right turn, look for an unmarked gravel road (CR 22 aka Spade Mine Rd) descending east. It's 1.5 mi. to the bottom. The last half is definitely HCV and may even require 4WD. Consult the topo for directions on reaching the individual holes on **Glade Creek**.

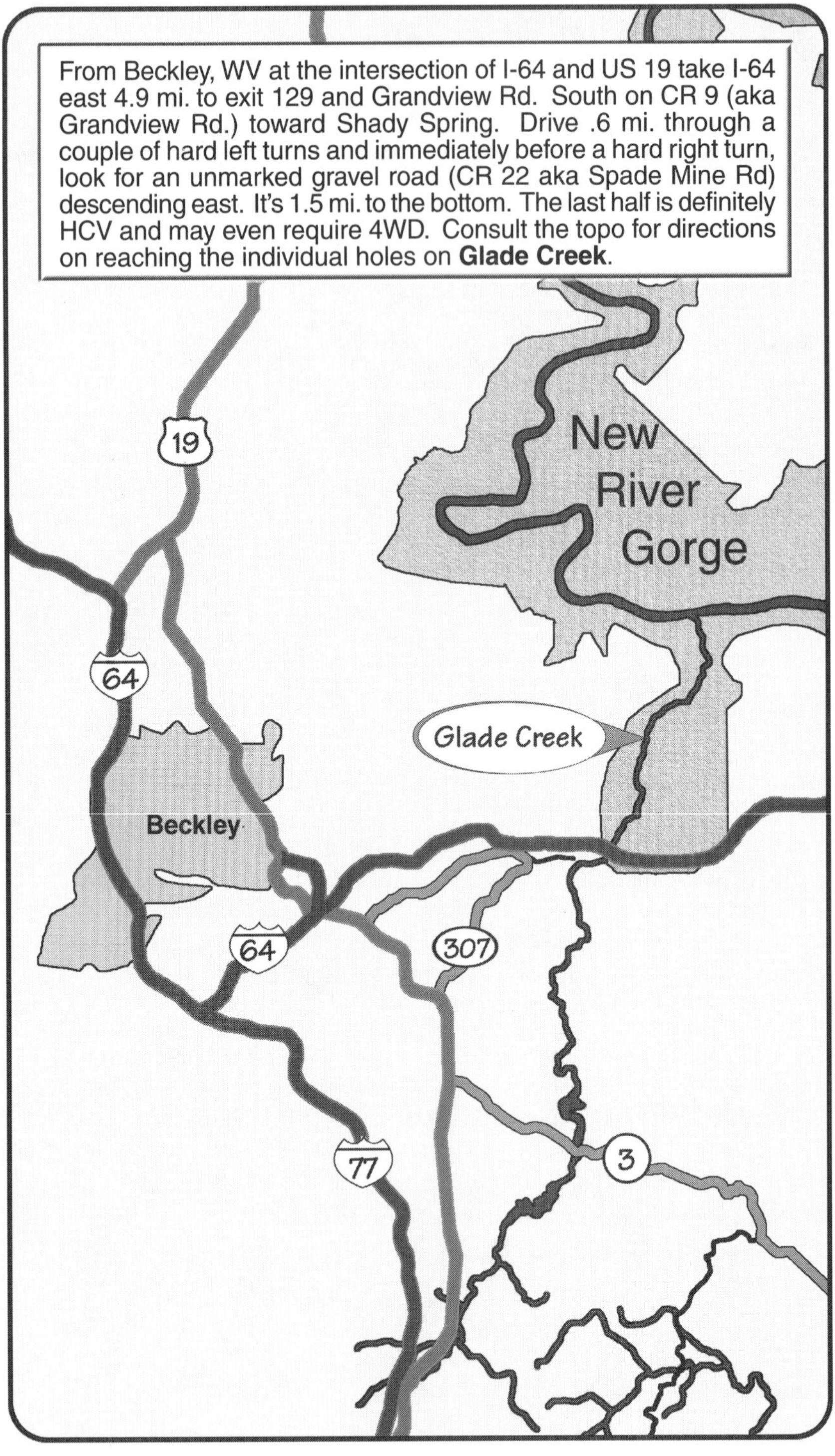

19

New River Gorge

64

Glade Creek

Beckley

64

307

77

3

One Fish

Probably the best place on the creek, the deepest anyway. Unlike the other falls on the Glade Creek, this one is not a wedding cake. It's a cascade that's cut an old fracture into a pretty little fan-shaped pool. The middle portion of the pool is completely unobstructed. It runs for approximately 30 feet. On the west side is a continuous, submerged ledge which is largely responsible for the depth. On the right is a nice sunning ledge three or four feet above the water.

The real star is the water quality. In this part of West Virginia it's really difficult to find something with visibility more than a couple of feet. But this is discharge from a reservoir. Plus there is hardly any settlement above it except a golf course which may let some nutrients into the watershed. Regardless, this is the best water quality I could find on the southern rim of the New River Gorge.

The pool is located right along the jeep trail and certainly gets some use. Scarcely any litter when I was there. It faces north so it may be a little cooler on very hot days.

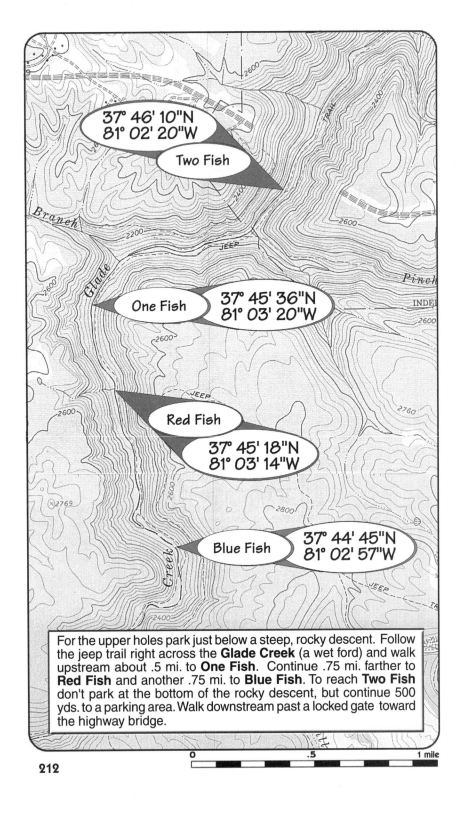

37° 46' 10"N
81° 02' 20"W

Two Fish

37° 45' 36"N
81° 03' 20"W

One Fish

Red Fish

37° 45' 18"N
81° 03' 14"W

Blue Fish

37° 44' 45"N
81° 02' 57"W

For the upper holes park just below a steep, rocky descent. Follow the jeep trail right across the **Glade Creek** (a wet ford) and walk upstream about .5 mi. to **One Fish**. Continue .75 mi. farther to **Red Fish** and another .75 mi. to **Blue Fish**. To reach **Two Fish** don't park at the bottom of the rocky descent, but continue 500 yds. to a parking area. Walk downstream past a locked gate toward the highway bridge.

0 .5 1 mile

Two Fish

A swimming hole under a highway bridge is hardly notable. The same conditions that produce many swimming holes — a narrow channel and solid rock on both sides — are the same places engineers prefer to build bridges. Furthermore, roads nearly always make the river too accessible, resulting in a bozo factor that's unacceptably high. This bridge is altogether different. It's 600 vertical feet above the creek, so it frames the feature, rather than polluting it.

The best view is from the upper pool. Water runs over a hard rock bed of Glade Creek to a broad, low ledge about 20 feet wide. Some of the sandstone is worn in a ripple pattern that looks like corduroy. The pool below is at least 40 feet long and framed at the bottom with small boulders and cobble. Not that deep, but there are a couple of places you will need to tread water. Plenty of shade. Not much seating.

A lower pool below the bridge has some boulders on the near side that create the cascade. It's about 25 to 30 feet long, but as much as one third of that is likely to be a stale eddy that forms behind a finger of hard rock stretching across the stream. The only good lounging, apart from a bench sized boulder, is the gravel bar on the far side. Very easy to get into and out of.

Red Fish

Red Fish

Small scale, but very pretty. The bed of Glade Creek above the pool is wide, exquisitely level and continuous, with few cracks or weakness. So the water, instead of draining into a couple of channels, spreads evenly over the breadth of the creek like icing over a sheet cake. The probable cause is a boundary of late Pennsylvanian rock from the Pocahontas Formation and Mississippian stone from the Bluestone and Princeton formation.

The jeep trail that parallels the creek can attract ATVs. Not the high throttle yahoos you find mud bogging in river beds. The trail isn't challenging enough for them. What you find instead are families traveling in pods like marine mammals. Dad takes point on the big red 450. The kids are in the middle on two-strike 250cc engines with blue smoke coming out the tail, and mom is riding sweeper on the 375 Mag.

Fortunately, the road surface on Glade Creek is really firm, some of it scratched out of solid rock, so the knobby tires don't hog it out except in a few soft spots. You won't find the litter normally associated with ATV access apart from the odd beer can and bait container.

Blue Fish

Blue Fish

Largest hole on Glade Creek. It's a two-tiered, scallop-shaped fall with gorgeous ledges on the left for sunning. A natural impound downstream maintains a depth of at least six feet, with water as deep as eight feet in places. The fall is probably 15 feet wide, depending on water level and the hole is 25 feet in diameter. No high vertical to dive from, more like low ledges where you can sit and dangle your toes in the water.

Lots of open sky. Upstream you can go explore the contours of the streambed, looking for small potholes and lounging spots in smooth, sculpted bedrock. Plenty of room to space out for privacy.

There are more charming water features along this stream. At one point between One Fish and Blue Fish the water rolls over an expanse of rock big enough to build a house on. A trough cut into the rock produces bath tubs, one of which is probably 12 feet long and about four and a half feet deep.

Kind of a steep scramble down to Blue Fish from the jeep trail. Sure footing is of benefit. If you get to a succession of three stream fords spaced closely together, then you went too far.

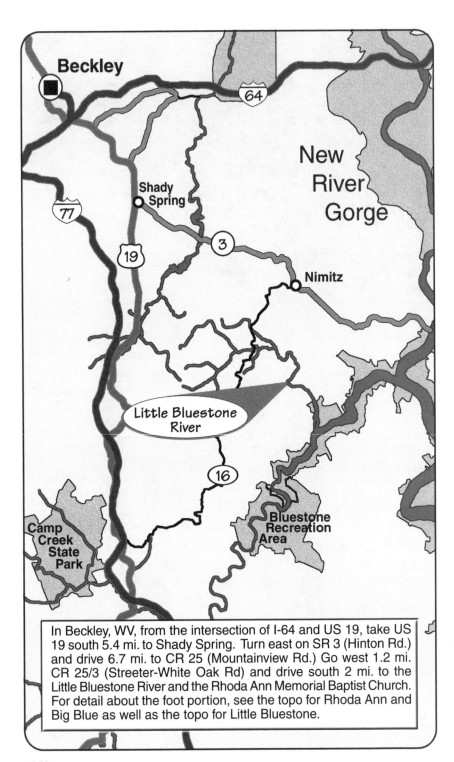

In Beckley, WV, from the intersection of I-64 and US 19, take US 19 south 5.4 mi. to Shady Spring. Turn east on SR 3 (Hinton Rd.) and drive 6.7 mi. to CR 25 (Mountainview Rd.) Go west 1.2 mi. CR 25/3 (Streeter-White Oak Rd) and drive south 2 mi. to the Little Bluestone River and the Rhoda Ann Memorial Baptist Church. For detail about the foot portion, see the topo for Rhoda Ann and Big Blue as well as the topo for Little Bluestone.

Rhoda Ann

An interesting blend of the sacred and the profane. A pool directly behind the Rhoda Ann Memorial Church has the prettiest conformation of just about any swimming hole I've seen. The container is very solid rock about 30 feet long and 12 feet wide. The water is seven to eight feet deep, but the really intriguing aesthetic is a submerged collar of sandstone that rings almost the entire pool. It creates the perfect place to stand in water up to your knees before you step off into the deep end. Great for baptisms. Jack Pack, a retired timberman, recounts services by the swimming hole.

"I can remember winters when we had to cut the ice off that pool to do the baptisms, yes I do."

Lots of country churches like Rhoda Ann, closed when parishioners either died off or raised enough money to build a brick church out on the state road. Today it's opened only for reunions and funerals. Now the trash barrel next to the baptismal pool is filled with beer cans and a couple of half-pint bottles.

I should have asked Pack how he felt about the hallowed spot making the transition from the Holy Spirit to the distilled variety. Instead I asked if winter baptisms in icy water wasn't uncomfortable.

"Son," he said, "when you're called to the Lord, temperature don't matter."

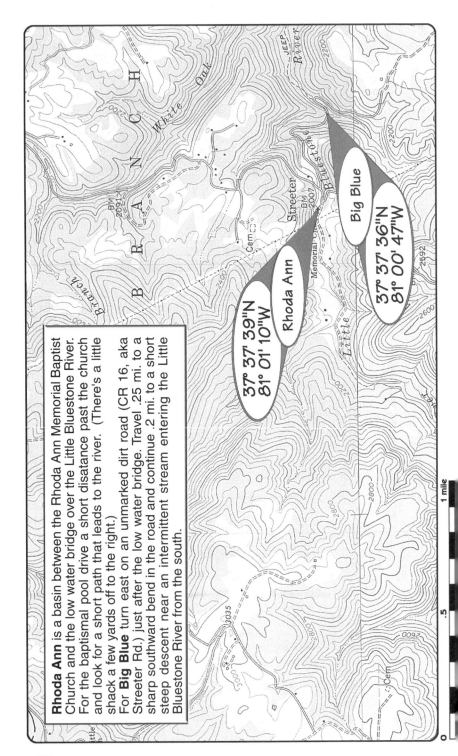

Rhoda Ann is a basin between the Rhoda Ann Memorial Baptist Church and the low water bridge over the Little Bluestone River. For the baptismal pool drive a short disatance past the church and look for a short path that leads to the river. (There's a little shack a few yards off to the right.)

For **Big Blue** turn east on an unmarked dirt road (CR 16, aka Streeter Rd.) just after the low water bridge. Travel .25 mi. to a sharp southward bend in the road and continue .2 mi. to a short steep descent near an intermittent stream entering the Little Bluestone River from the south.

Rhoda Ann

37° 37' 39"N
81° 01' 10"W

Big Blue

37° 37' 36"N
81° 00' 47"W

1 mile

.5

0

Big Blue

Generations have ridden the rope swing at this pale green swimming hole on the Little Bluestone River. It happens within a formation of blue gray shale and sandstone. Very pretty how the creek slides along in a low-angle cascade, cutting a beautiful sinuous line before it hits softer rock. The differential erosion produces an oval shaped container about 50 feet long and perhaps 30 feet wide. It's deeply shaded by hard woods, many of which have toppled over in the loose soil. Fortunately, there's at least one tree sturdy enough for the rope where Gino Moye spent his summer vacations.

"All of my grandparents are from Nimitz," Moye says. "I grew up in Idaho, but we used to come back for family reunions and we'd go to that swimming hole."

Something about water in the Little Bluestone fosters aquatic aggression. Moye ended up as a Navy SEAL and when he brings his own son back to West Virginia the pattern repeats.

"My boy loved it. A real water hound. He scares the hell out of me."

Now, the bad part. Visibility is no more than three feet. Lots of vehicular activity, too. The road is a real mud bog in places. Level at an upstream gauge was 220 cfs when this photo was taken.

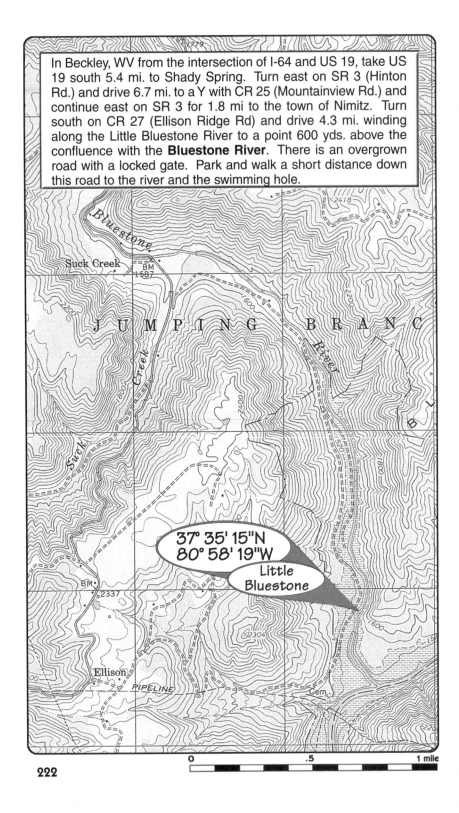

In Beckley, WV from the intersection of I-64 and US 19, take US 19 south 5.4 mi. to Shady Spring. Turn east on SR 3 (Hinton Rd.) and drive 6.7 mi. to a Y with CR 25 (Mountainview Rd.) and continue east on SR 3 for 1.8 mi to the town of Nimitz. Turn south on CR 27 (Ellison Ridge Rd) and drive 4.3 mi. winding along the Little Bluestone River to a point 600 yds. above the confluence with the **Bluestone River**. There is an overgrown road with a locked gate. Park and walk a short distance down this road to the river and the swimming hole.

37° 35' 15"N
80° 58' 19"W

Little
Bluestone

0   .5   1 mile

Little Bluestone

Not the Little Bluestone swimming hole favored by every beer guzzling, monster truck mud bogger in Summers County. This is a place tucked up around a corner from there. It's a horseshoe shaped pool against a small outcrop of what appears to be some flaky limestone. The river, which is usually less than five feet wide, broadens considerably. It's cut one deep notch into the limestone that makes a deeply shaded pool, good on the hottest days.

The entire 80-foot length of the wall is trimmed in a lovely scalloped edge. The rock reaches its height at about 10 feet. You'll be able to float and paddle around below the ledge, but it's not likely to be deep enough to jump into. This is more of a lazy afternoon spot.

Opposite the rock there will be a nice sand beach during lower levels. And of course the ledges are a lovely place to toss a blanket. An old fire ring and some pit scars indicate that some people do come here, but it's very lightly visited compared with much of the rest of the Bluestone Public Hunting and Fishing Area.

Note: the last portion of the drive is dirt road. HCV recommended. If it's wet, you'll be better off with 4-wheel drive.

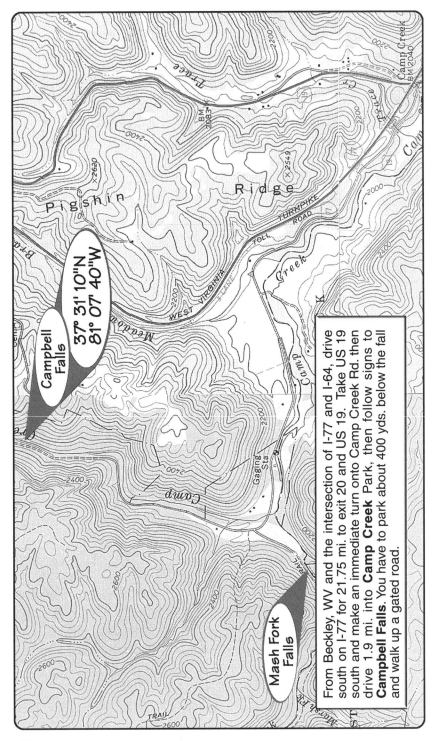

Campbell Falls

37° 31' 10"N
81° 07' 40"W

Mash Fork Falls

From Beckley, WV and the intersection of I-77 and I-64, drive south on I-77 for 21.75 mi. to exit 20 and US 19. Take US 19 south and make an immediate turn onto Camp Creek Rd. then drive 1.9 mi. into **Camp Creek** Park, then follow signs to **Campbell Falls**. You have to park about 400 yds. below the fall and walk up a gated road.

Campbell Fall

The best high water spot in this part of the state. The multi-tiered fall face is 50 feet wide and the pool below is very broad given the size of the stream. That means it takes lots of water to fill it up. Glorious ledges to relax on, but with the picnic area and campground less than one mile away, privacy is not to be had.

Looking at a map you may notice that several place names in the park refer to the area's moonshine heritage. The illicit craft can still produce minor leg injuries for overland hikers. After whiskey barrels rot the iron bands remain camouflaged in decades of leaf litter until someone steps on one and it pops up to whack them in the knee.

"Just about any branch you go up there was somebody cooking," said Curtis Laxton, a park employee. Laxton pedaled his grandfather's moonshine — literally.

"I used to ride around and do deliveries on a 28-inch Mohawk. I was just eight and I couldn't even reach the pedals on a bike that big. I had to wait 'till the pedal came up to the top of the stroke and push it down halfway until the opposite pedal came around to the top."

Nearly all the watershed is within the state park and water quality on Camp Creek is excellent. Maybe that's why it made such good 'shine.

For **Cascades** start in Blacksburg, VA at the northern jct. of US 460 and business 460 (aka North Main St.) and drive west on US 460 for 14 mi. to the town of Pembroke and Cascade Drive. Turn north 3.25 mi. to the parking for Cascades Fall.

For **Dismal** drive south on US 460 from Blacksburg, VA. to I-81. Turn west for 15.6 mi. to SR 100. Turn north for 11.7 mi., then west on SR 42. Drive 10.3 mi. to CR 606. Turn north .9 mi. to CR 201 and another .9 mi. to roadside parking.

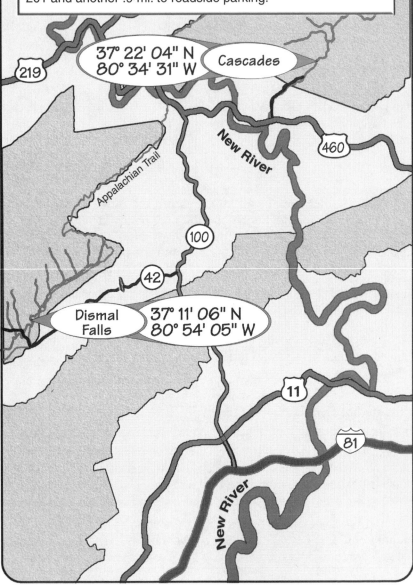

37° 22' 04" N
80° 34' 31" W   Cascades

Appalachian Trail

New River

460

100

42

Dismal
Falls   37° 11' 06" N
80° 54' 05" W

11

81

New River

Cascades Falls

Gorgeous fall. Big damn pool.

Water comes off a wafer thin ledge that overhangs the wall by three to five feet. That creates a plunge fall for about 20 feet until, at about the hallway point, the water explodes onto a belly of slate and scatters into a pool about 60 feet long and 30 to 40 feet wide. The sandstone forming the pool is certainly overhead deep and better, but depth is really immaterial, because there's nothing to jump from. Nothing vertical, anyway. The entire eastern side of the hole is comprised of bed rock that's just under the water's surface. It arcs all the way around to the fall. For a dive you could wade over to some submerged slabs adjoining the fail. It's around ankle deep, but then you'd be jumping out of the water in order to jump in the water and that's just not as satisfying as catching air.

During the summer there will be at least one club van from a summer camp or youth outing parked at the trailhead. Fortunately there is ample space to spread out around the pool. The fall faces south so there is good sun.

I spent a Saturday afternoon there and often when a guy gets to the top of the 50-foot fall, he hollers Woooohoooo!" Lots of that at Cascades Falls.

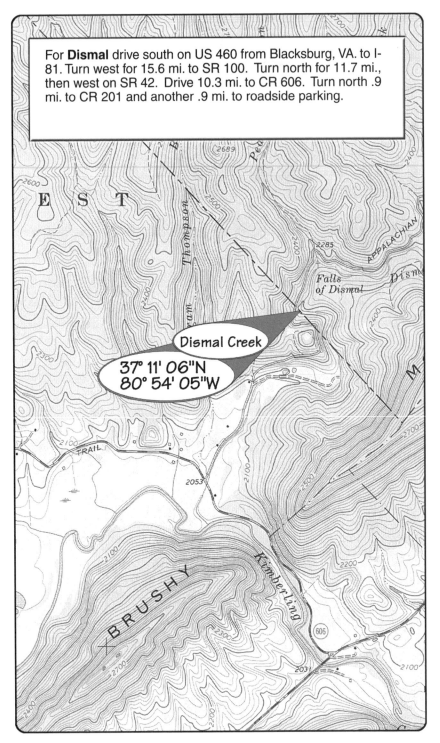

For **Dismal** drive south on US 460 from Blacksburg, VA. to I-81. Turn west for 15.6 mi. to SR 100. Turn north for 11.7 mi., then west on SR 42. Drive 10.3 mi. to CR 606. Turn north .9 mi. to CR 201 and another .9 mi. to roadside parking.

Dismal Creek

37° 11' 06"N
80° 54' 05"W

Dismal Creek

A popular spot where Dismal Creek bounds over a highly stratified sandstone ledge and into a hole about 40 feet long. There's a sweet spot 20 feet by 10 feet wide, meaning you can jump from the top of the ledge for a ride of eight vertical feet. Southern exposure means that Dismal warms early in the season and stays open late. Limited seating at the bottom, but lots of room to relax up at the top. The Appalachian Trail parallels the entire length of the creek.

However, access on the county road can attract drunken idiots and broken glass. Cleanup is effected by an unlikely Boy Scout with black toenails, an imposing necklace made of boar's tusks and a Confederate battle flag. He's Brian Pauley, a Tar Heel transplant to the Old Dominion who does volunteer cleanup while offering unprintable opinions about how people in Jiles County take care of their natural places.

"I've been here five times this week," he said during a break. "There was an awful mess. It took me eight trash bags to collect all the junk that (irresponsible) people left behind, stuff that'd been lying around here for years."

Pauley uses a broom to sweep the rock for glass, but you should not walk barefoot here.

Brush Creek

37° 27' 57"N
81° 03' 41"W

Very pretty fall and a rope swing. Water smelled nasty...and they say it's actually gotten better.

Eads Mill

37° 28' 44"N
81° 04' 17"W

Redneck hangout. Some of the worst litter I've seen.

Mash Fork

37° 30' 04"N
81° 08' 34"W

In Camp Creek State Park. Water doesn't pool enough to be a swimming hole. Interesting rock, though.

Suck Creek

37° 36' 03"N
80° 59' 15"W

A short, broad fall fills a pool about 30-feet wide. Deep end is close to six feet. Almost worth a visit based on the name alone.

Cotton Hill

38° 06' 59"N
81° 08' 41"W

An ashtray. This is a roadside spot along US 60. Cigarettes butts collect in small depressions in the rock, and after a rain remain floating for days.

Greenbrier River

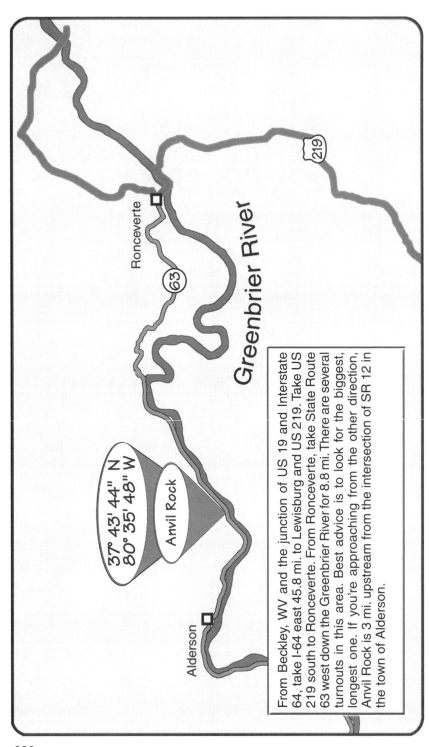

Greenbrier River

Roncoverte

63

219

37° 43' 44" N
80° 35' 48" W

Anvil Rock

Alderson

From Beckley, WV and the junction of US 19 and Interstate 64, take I-64 east 45.8 mi. to Lewisburg and US 219. Take US 219 south to Ronceverte. From Ronceverte, take State Route 63 west down the Greenbrier River for 8.8 mi. There are several turnouts in this area. Best advice is to look for the biggest, longest one. If you're approaching from the other direction, Anvil Rock is 3 mi. upstream from the intersection of SR 12 in the town of Alderson.

Anvil Rock

Roadside cliff diving. Anvil Rock is a big hunk of limestone about the size of one of those double box cars rolling down the rail line on the opposite shore of the Greenbrier River. It's taller — as high 19 feet and it's pointed into the deep, main channel of the river. Most natives of Alderson, a picturesque railroad town downstream, can remember the first time they jumped off of the rock.

"The first time I went I must have been 12," said Jack Still, a municipal judge. "The first of May every year, we'd skip school and go swimming. We didn't give a damn if there was snow on the ground, we went. And no swimming suits were involved."

Time has passed. State Route 63 is paved and Jack Still is old enough that he's retired from not one, but two careers. Attitudes about skinny dipping have changed also. Asked about contemporary standards, the city judge pauses and says, "All I ask is that if people are going to skinny dip that they do it outside the city limits."

Anvil Rock a regular party spot. It was clean when I visited only one case of empties sitting on the shoulder. Water quality is marginal as you might expect on the main stem of a major river. There's just a whole lot of everything upstream.

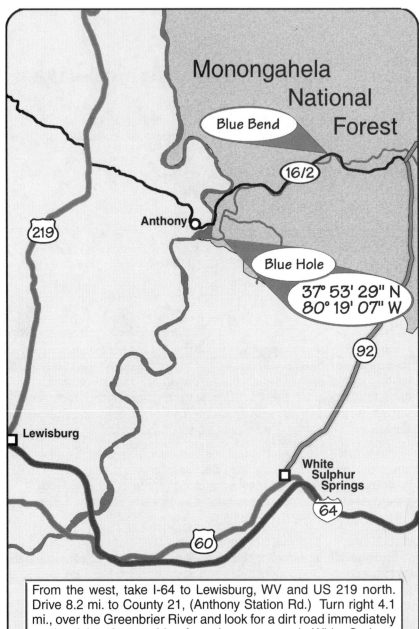

Monongahela National Forest

Blue Bend

16/2

Anthony

219

Blue Hole

37° 53' 29" N
80° 19' 07" W

92

Lewisburg

White
Sulphur
Springs

64

60

From the west, take I-64 to Lewisburg, WV and US 219 north. Drive 8.2 mi. to County 21, (Anthony Station Rd.) Turn right 4.1 mi., over the Greenbrier River and look for a dirt road immediately on the right. Approaching from the east, start in White Springs, WV and drive north on SR 92 for 9.15 mi. to SR 16/2, aka Big Blue Bend Rd. Turn left. It's 7.8 mi. west to the South Boundary Trailhead. See the follofing topo for hiking directions.
Note: You'll pass Blue Bend Recreation Area. Very pretty spot.

Blue Hole

With its Parkhead member and Foreknob formation, conglomeratic interbeds never looked so sexy. We are of course talking about a geologic formation, one of the upper Devonian era, that butts up against some earlier rocks to produce a couple of swimming holes on Anthony Creek. These different geologic structures along the Allegheny Front influence Anthony Creek even more than most watersheds in the eastern part of the state.

In this case, a knife-edge ridge of gray sandstone from the Mississipian era forces Anthony Creek into a hard turn and over a finger of softer Hampshire formation about .75 miles upstream. (See following page) Near Blue Hole, the creek reaches the southern extent of a narrow, north-south expression of this Hampshire formation that starts way up in the Dolly Sods Wilderness. The creek rounds the end of the ridge and bounces off the north flank of Greenbrier Mountain shortly before entering the river of the same name.

The swimming hole is a slow, lazy channel 150 feet long and, depending on water level, 15 to 25 feet wide. There's no impound at the bottom, so depth won't be great. There is a small outcrop of bedrock across from a sand, mud and gravel beach. Water quality is cloudy.

The place is fairly well known and at about .75 miles from the parking area, it's not beyond beer cooler distance.

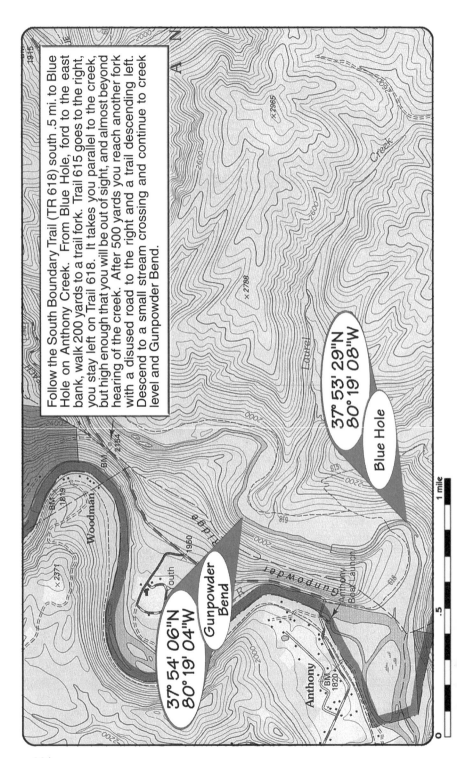

Follow the South Boundary Trail (TR 618) south .5 mi. to Blue Hole on Anthony Creek. From Blue Hole, ford to the east bank, walk 200 yards to a trail fork. Trail 615 goes to the right, you stay left on Trail 618. It takes you parallel to the creek, but high enough that you will be out of sight, and almost beyond hearing of the creek. After 500 yards you reach another fork with a disused road to the right and a trail descending left. Descend to a small stream crossing and continue to creek level and Gunpowder Bend.

37° 53' 29"N
80° 19' 08""W

Blue Hole

37° 54' 06"N
80° 19' 04""W

Gunpowder Bend

1 mile

.5

0

236

Gunpowder Bend

This part of Anthony Creek is lined with cobble and boulders. The result is not a bodacious swimming hole. There's no waterfall, no pool with sinuous lines, nothing to jump from. It *is* a place far enough from the trailhead to filter out most bozos. A place with a good mix of sun and shade, a pool deep enough that you have to tread water, some good spots to camp and a picnic table. If Gunpowder Bend were food, it would be a burger with fries. Which is to say simple and satisfying.

From Blue Hole, ford to the east bank, walk 200 yards or so to a trail fork. Trail 615 goes to the right, you stay left on Trail 618. It takes you parallel to the creek, but high enough that you will be out of sight, and almost beyond hearing of the water. After 500 yards you reach another fork with an unused road to the right and a trail descending left. Descend, crossing a small stream and continue to creek level.

Note that 200 yards upstream from the highway saddle is a long slow pool. It's worth mentioning, but not quite worth a separate review. It's best located by finding a huge hemlock more than 36 inches in diameter. Another 400 yards after that the creek becomes accessible from the road.

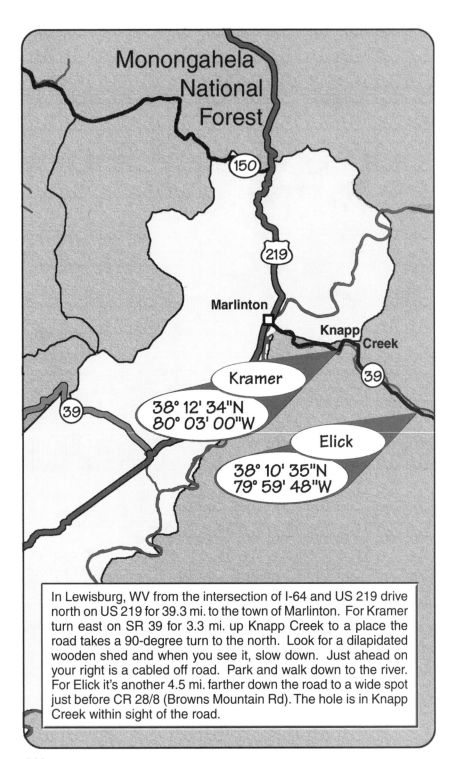

Monongahela National Forest

150

219

Marlinton

Knapp Creek

39

Kramer

38° 12' 34"N
80° 03' 00"W

39

Elick

38° 10' 35"N
79° 59' 48"W

In Lewisburg, WV from the intersection of I-64 and US 219 drive north on US 219 for 39.3 mi. to the town of Marlinton. For Kramer turn east on SR 39 for 3.3 mi. up Knapp Creek to a place the road takes a 90-degree turn to the north. Look for a dilapidated wooden shed and when you see it, slow down. Just ahead on your right is a cabled off road. Park and walk down to the river. For Elick it's another 4.5 mi. farther down the road to a wide spot just before CR 28/8 (Browns Mountain Rd). The hole is in Knapp Creek within sight of the road.

Knapp Creek

A couple of easy access spots on a tributary to the Greenbrier River. Very local. Generations of Pocahantas County residents have come here to refresh themselves. The better pool is called Elick. Here you'll find a couple of medium sized boulders opposite one another. The one on the far side is about six feet off the water. Historically it had a diving board bolted on top via a set of automobile leaf springs.

Together with a low band of adjoining stone, the rock forces a bend in the river that's probably 45 feet long and 15 feet across. Litter hardly seemed a problem and given the proximity to the road. That suggests somebody picks it up regularly.

Five miles downstream is another place called Kramer. It's got a riffle at the top and a riffle at the bottom. In between is at least 100 feet of water that in places is chin deep on the average NBA player. None of the stream morphology indicates there would be anything of interest here. It occurs at a flat place in the river with an undistinguished bank, just mud and rocks. Water quality is fair; some foam on the top and turbidity limits visibility to around four feet. That'll vary with temperature, season and even weather. Litter at the trailhead includes chewing tobacco pouches and fishing lures.

Blue Bend

37° 55' 19"N
80° 15' 52"W

Of the half dozen or so swimming holes that have "blue" in their names, this is the only one that actually appears a little blue. It's a wide turn in Anthony Creek right next to the road. Thousands of visitors annually.

Lindsay Slide

37° 37' 52"N
80° 45' 47"W

On the main stem of the Greenbrier River amidst a community of mainly ramshackle cabins. No place to park and some question of whether there's right of way for the public.

Turn Hole

37° 36' 43"N
80° 45' 58"W

On the main stem of the Greenbrier River. Posted. Appears to be private.

Potomac Highlands & Shenandoah Park

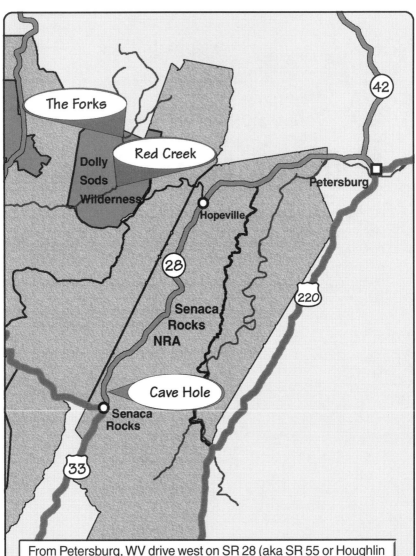

The Forks

Red Creek

Dolly
Sods
Wilderness

Petersburg

Hopeville

28

Senaca
Rocks
NRA

Cave Hole

Senaca
Rocks

33

42

220

From Petersburg, WV drive west on SR 28 (aka SR 55 or Houghlin Ln) for 9.2 mi. along the North Fork South Branch of the Potomac River. At an intersection just before the village of Hopeville, make a 120-degree turn north and drive .8 mi. to FS 19 in the Monongahela National Forest. Go west on FS 19 for 6 mi. to FS 75 and the Dolly Sods Wilderness. See 24K map for further directions.

For **Cave Hole** start at the intersection of US 33 and SR 28. Drive north a couple of hundred feet to the entrance for Seneca Rocks picnic grounds. Bear left to the lower parking area and hike the short gravel path to the river.

Forks of Red Creek

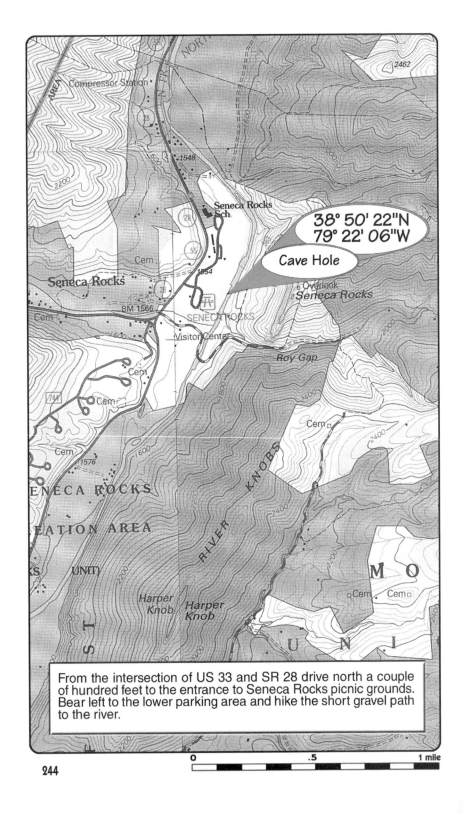

38° 50' 22"N
79° 22' 06"W

Cave Hole

From the intersection of US 33 and SR 28 drive north a couple of hundred feet to the entrance to Seneca Rocks picnic grounds. Bear left to the lower parking area and hike the short gravel path to the river.

0 .5 1 mile

Photo: Sarah Fellows

Cave Hole

A family spot about 150 feet long. The best part is where the North Fork South Branch Potomac River bumps up against some of the bedrock and makes a deep hole. The rest of the water stretches more than 100 feet downstream in a placid basin. There's a large gravel beach deeply shaded with sycamore and several rock perches on the other side of the river at the bottom of the crag. The namesake cave is bored into the rock over there. Difficult to find, but fun to look for.

Above is Seneca Rocks, one of the most recognizable features in West Virginia. It's a formation of very hard Tuscarora sandstone that was uplifted and eroded over 400 million years until it looks like a pale dorsal fin rising 900 feet above the North Fork South Branch Potomac River. It appears incongruous among the moderately sloped, mixed forests of eastern West Virginia, but several similar formations dot the landscape, they're little known and less visited because they're on private land.

Seneca Rocks has been a Mecca for eastern rock climbers for decades. The Monongahela National Forest recently the Forest Service built a plush visitor's center to accommodate sightseers. There's so much parking around it, so many signs that say Seneca Rocks that the swimming hole a little difficult to find.

From FS 75 you can drive north 3.2 mi. to the Red Creek Trail. Descend TR 510 for 900 vertical feet over 2 mi. staying right along Fischer Spring Run. Continue downstream 200 yds. for the lower fall. The middle and upper falls are 200 yds and 400 yds. north, respectively. Alternately, you can start at the bottom of the Dolly Sods Wilderness. Pass FS 75 and descend 3.6 mi. to Red Creek and the southern entrance for Dolly Sods Wilderness. Hike 2.7 mi. north along the Red Creek Trail.

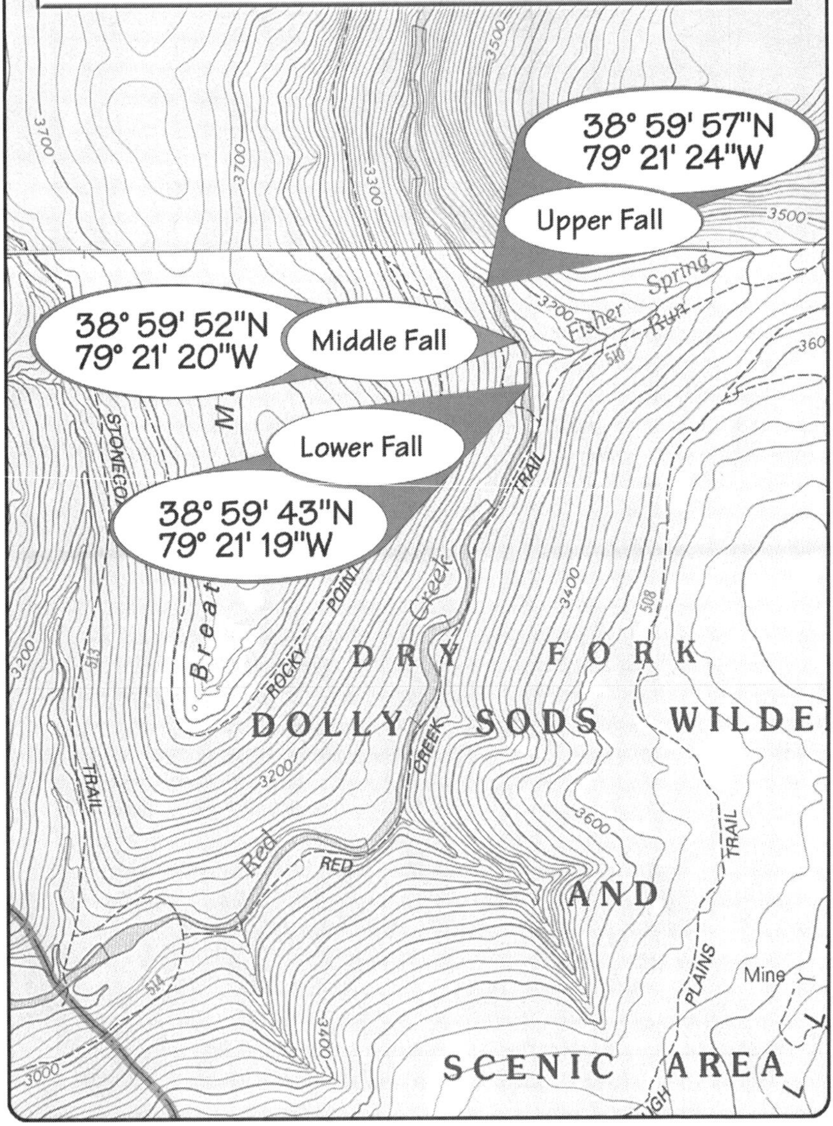

38° 59' 57"N
79° 21' 24"W

Upper Fall

38° 59' 52"N
79° 21' 20"W

Middle Fall

Lower Fall

38° 59' 43"N
79° 21' 19"W

DRY FORK

DOLLY SODS WILDE

AND

SCENIC AREA

Lower Fall

A couple of spots in the Dolly Sods Wilderness formed in finely bedded, brittle stone. The rock is aligned on the same plane as the water flow on Red Creek, so it's smooth rather than badly fractured as you might expect from such stone. At the lower fall, water comes off the lip in a couple of broad scallops. The pool below is modest, about 10 feet long and not quite as wide. Not much size, but pretty and lots of sun with close to 1,000 square feet of slabs relax on. If you have a Teflon tailbone you might test it for water slide suitability, but it looked marginal for that use.

Upstream is a slightly higher fall, a little more rambunctious and more blocky. It's not as pretty, doesn't have the aesthetics of the downstream fall, however the pool is far bigger and much deeper. This, because there is a hole at the bottom of the fall that catches all the rock and leaves the swimming hole unobstructed and deep. Not nearly as much sky as its downstream cousin, plus it's east facing so it gets cool in the afternoon.

Stern Warning: Do not plan overnight trips in this part of the Mononga-hela National Forest. You're not supposed to camp so close to water, for starters. In addition heavy visitorship and campfires have damaged the area. It's bad enough that people unconcerned about the environment are spoiling watersheds; it's worse when people who should care are doing the same thing.

Photo: Sarah Fellows

Upper Falls

Unlike the ledge falls below, this is a cascade into a modest, parallel-sided pool about 25 feet long that gets eight feet deep. That empties onto a large slab about the size of a dance floor. Best when water levels on Red Creek are higher. On the eastern side is a nice little stack of rock. The best thing this has going for it is privacy. It doesn't seem to get lots of people, even though the trail on the western side is pretty apparent. There's potential rump bumping above the cascade with relatively smooth rock running for 150 to 200 feet. The angle is kind of shallow, though. There's also a pocket of sand about the size of a double bed.

Perhaps more interesting than the swimming holes is the wildlife, specifically the number of deer in the Monongahela National Forest and its surroundings. In the evening it's not unusual to see 40 or 50 deer grazing on a hillside. They're not plentiful, but since they're in the wilderness they're not hunted and as such are very passive.

One man from Elkins said that during a boyhood trip into the Dolly Sods Wilderness she carried a wooden hiking stick. Each time he got close enough to a deer to throw it and hit the deer, he carved a notch in the handle. At the end of five days he had seven notches in his stick.

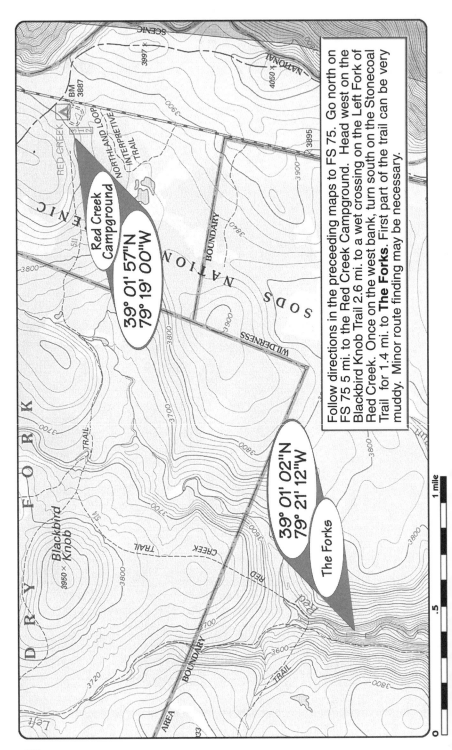

Follow directions in the preceeding maps to FS 75. Go north on FS 75 5 mi. to the Red Creek Campground. Head west on the Blackbird Knob Trail 2.6 mi. to a wet crossing on the Left Fork of Red Creek. Once on the west bank, turn south on the Stonecoal Trail for 1.4 mi. to **The Forks**. First part of the trail can be very muddy. Minor route finding may be necessary.

Red Creek Campground
39° 01' 57"N
79° 19' 00"W

The Forks
39° 01' 02"N
79° 21' 12"W

1 mile

.5

The Forks

Three features in close succession. The best is the second one. Here's the rundown: At the top a confluence widens into a basin about seventy feet long. It's formed mainly by freestone, hence not very deep, but there is a smashing sand beach just up the Left Fork of Red Creek where you can stretch out for a siesta.

The lower swimming hole is the lesser of the three. It's a scramble getting there and significant intrusion from boulders limits the surface area of the pool. Plus, it doesn't get much sunlight. It's probably only good on hot days during a dry spell.

But the middle is a classic. Some very hard rock lines the bed of the creek. It's interrupted in a few places by slots of softer stone that get worn away and produce deep undercuts in the form of headward erosion. Water pours off in a low plunge across a beautiful sheet twenty feet wide. It's cut back under the fall lip by four or five feet. Interesting, but not meaningful. What's important is a similar lip downstream, opposite the fall face. It forces downward rushing water into a hydraulic that digs deeper and deeper into the bottom of the pool. Difficult to explain, but when you see it, you'll understand.

The water apparently has few nutrients in it, hence no algae. It is however dark red from the tannins vegetation in the Dolly Sods Widerness. The color has the red brick appearance of a very old, very fine wine.

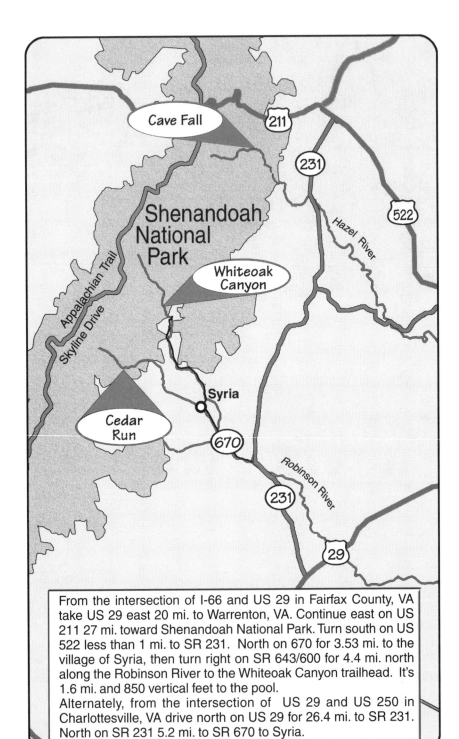

Cave Fall

211

231

522

Shenandoah
National
Park

Hazel River

Appalachian Trail

Skyline Drive

Whiteoak
Canyon

Cedar
Run

Syria

670

Robinson River

231

29

From the intersection of I-66 and US 29 in Fairfax County, VA take US 29 east 20 mi. to Warrenton, VA. Continue east on US 211 27 mi. toward Shenandoah National Park. Turn south on US 522 less than 1 mi. to SR 231. North on 670 for 3.53 mi. to the village of Syria, then turn right on SR 643/600 for 4.4 mi. north along the Robinson River to the Whiteoak Canyon trailhead. It's 1.6 mi. and 850 vertical feet to the pool.
Alternately, from the intersection of US 29 and US 250 in Charlottesville, VA drive north on US 29 for 26.4 mi. to SR 231. North on SR 231 5.2 mi. to SR 670 to Syria.

Pro Tour

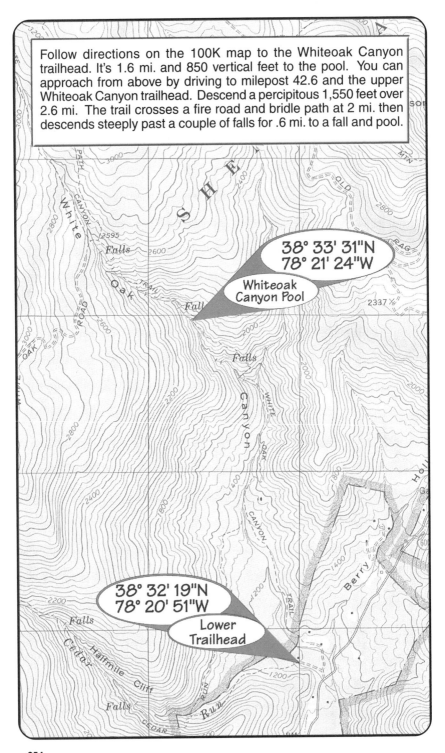

Follow directions on the 100K map to the Whiteoak Canyon trailhead. It's 1.6 mi. and 850 vertical feet to the pool. You can approach from above by driving to milepost 42.6 and the upper Whiteoak Canyon trailhead. Descend a percipitous 1,550 feet over 2.6 mi. The trail crosses a fire road and bridle path at 2 mi. then descends steeply past a couple of falls for .6 mi. to a fall and pool.

38° 33' 31"N
78° 21' 24"W

Whiteoak Canyon Pool

38° 32' 19"N
78° 20' 51"W

Lower Trailhead

White Oak Canyon

There are six waterfalls between the bottom of White Oak Canyon and Skyline Drive. However only one fall that's accessible from the main trail is a good swimming hole. The trail follows blue blazes into Shenandoah National Park. A couple of hundred feet after the parking area it forks. You stay right.

After one mile and 250 vertical feet you come to a modest basin. It's a good scale for kids who just took the training wheels off their bike. The next stop is an impressive couple of falls just above a confluence entering from the right, or about 1.35 miles in. The fall is a horsetail 30 feet high with a pool about 55 feet wide. Depth is lacking due to rock fall and snags. From there the trail climbs steeply toward the swimming hole that I like.

It's a rocky pool, roughly oval in shape and about 20 feet long. Loads of debris rafted up at the bottom improves the depth. Problem is there's no place to sit or get comfortable. You could probably swim over to the short cascade that feeds the pool and haul out on some smooth rocks there. Other rocks are very slippery. Definitely wear sandals or water shoes. A walking stick is also an excellent idea.

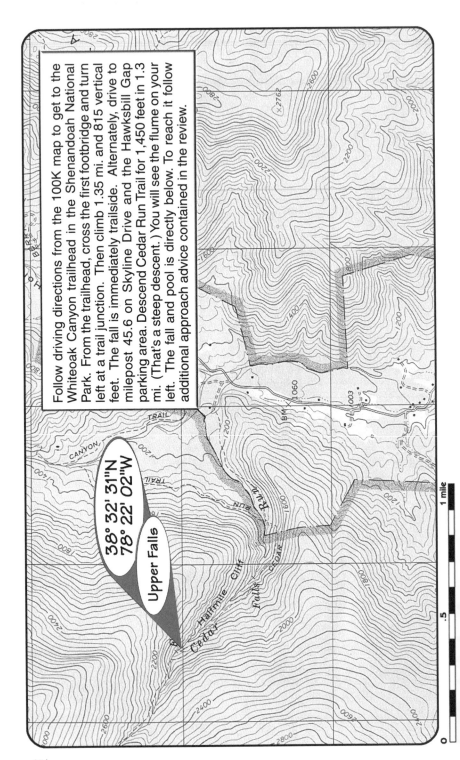

Follow driving directions from the 100K map to get to the Whiteoak Canyon trailhead in the Shenandoah National Park. From the trailhead, cross the first footbridge and turn left at a trail junction. Then climb 1.35 mi. and 815 vertical feet. The fall is immediately trailside. Alternately, drive to milepost 45.6 on Skyline Drive and the Hawksbill Gap parking area. Descend Cedar Run Trail for 1,450 feet in 1.3 mi. (That's a steep descent.) You will see the flume on your left. The fall and pool is directly below. To reach it follow additional approach advice contained in the review.

38° 32' 31"N
78° 22' 02"W

Upper Falls

Cedar Run

It's a steep, narrow hole more than forty feet high on the right side. A long, twisting slot cuts a shallow trough into the rock until the creek reaches a void then leaps over the lip. Water is correspondingly deep at the bottom, but nothing to jump from and not lots of surface area to aim for even if there was. The pool is five feet wide where the fall enters and no more than ten feet wide at the discharge. Plus there is a cleaver shaped rock in the middle. One misplaced dive and it would split you in two.

There's almost no horizontal component at all. Just a couple of benches and boulders to sit on. It might seat three or four people. The value of this swimming hole is as refuge on the hottest days in the driest season. If Northern Virginia turned into the Gobi Desert, there would still be water in the bottom of this hole. It's so dark and cool that a vampire could party all day without sunblock.

It takes a good pair of legs to hike the length of the trail. It's a wicked 2,260 vertical feet to the top at Skyline Drive and this place is about one-third of the way up. This is a popular trail in Shenandoah National Park and you can be certain that lots of people peep over the lip of the fall into the hole, so forget about privacy. But comparatively few will make the trip down into it.

Be advised if you use a GPS receiver that signals in this canyon may vary considerably.

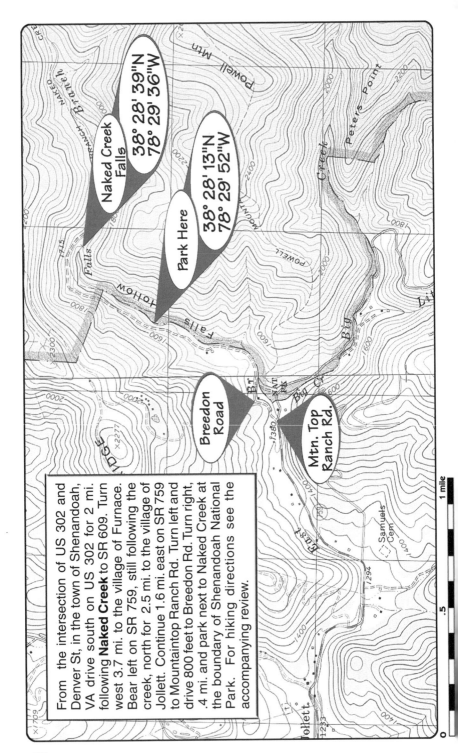

From the intersection of US 302 and Denver St, in the town of Shenandoah, VA drive south on US 302 for 2 mi. following **Naked Creek** to SR 609. Turn west 3.7 mi. to the village of Furnace. Bear left on SR 759, still following the creek, north for 2.5 mi. to the village of Jollett. Continue 1.6 mi. east on SR 759 to Mountaintop Ranch Rd. Turn left and drive 800 feet to Breedon Rd. Turn right, .4 mi. and park next to Naked Creek at the boundary of Shenandoah National Park. For hiking directions see the accompanying review.

Naked Creek Falls

38° 28' 39"N
78° 29' 36"W

Park Here

38° 28' 13"N
78° 29' 52"W

Breedon Road

Mtn. Top Ranch Rd.

0   .5   1 mile

Naked Creek

At the lower fall you'll find a collar of rock about twelve feet high with a cascade about eight feet tall. The pool at the bottom is approximately forty feet wide and about twenty feet long and nine feet at its deepest. Nothing you can jump from. The other deficiency is lack of anyplace to sit. Lots of vegetation like poplar, beech, chinkapin and sycamore. Plenty of wide-open sky with lots of sunshine in the afternoon. You'll be able to jump in this cool water, get out and dry off in the sun.

Upstream is a taller fall with a smaller pool. An abandoned logging road goes along the rim of a bowl 80 feet wide with the fall and pool below. Pretty impressive view. The fall is a twenty-foot horsetail. Depth is a little better than six feet because of all the stones and cobble.

Getting to the trailhead requires lots of confusing turns. See the map on the left for details. The trailhead isn't marked, either. Most people walk through a gate, past a "No Trespassing" sign and follow the creek upstream to the fall. You may park just to the right of a white frame house, then take an ATV trail uphill to the left. Climb for 360 vertical feet over .3 miles then bear left and climb another 140 vertical feet to a junction with a logging road that contours east. Soon that road/trail begins a descent toward Naked Creek. As you get down toward the creek the trail crosses another couple of roads. Pick the downhill direction at each junction.

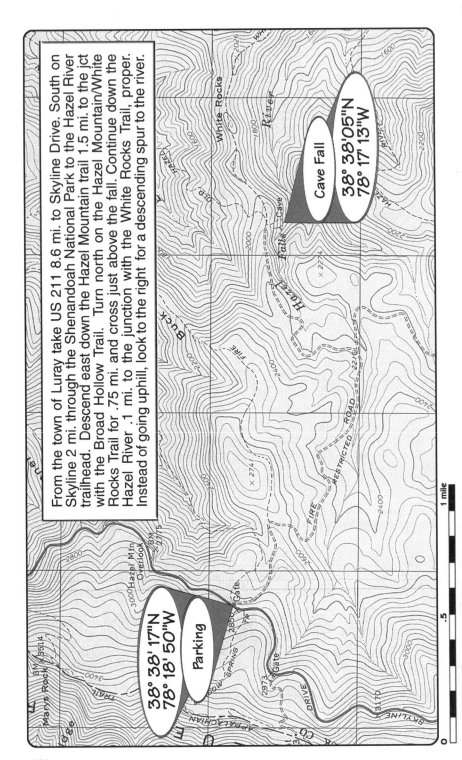

From the town of Luray take US 211 8.6 mi. to Skyline Drive. South on Skyline 2 mi. through the Shenandoah National Park to the Hazel River trailhead. Descend east down the Hazel Mountain trail 1.5 mi. to the jct with the Broad Hollow Trail. Turn north on the Hazel Mountain/White Rocks Trail for .75 mi. and cross just above the fall. Continue down the Hazel River .1 mi. to the junction with the White Rocks Trail, proper. Instead of going uphill, look to the right for a descending spur to the river.

Cave Fall
38° 38'05"N
78° 17'13"W

Parking
38° 38'17"N
78° 18'50"W

0   .5   1 mile

Cave Falls

A tub so straight and square that Pythagoras would have been the first one to pull off his tunic and dive in. He might bump his Greek forehead on Virginia sandstone. The pool is small, less than less 20 feet long, about eight feet wide at the top and ten feet wide at the bottom where an anvil shaped rock has dropped into the stream, creating the impound. This spot where the Hazel River runs through Shenandoah National Park isn't that deep, but the pool's beautiful trapezoidal dimensions make it look like something that could be in a suburban backyard with a barbecue kettle parked next to it.

The pool is well below the fall itself, which is an outstanding setting, but not worth mentioning as a swimming hole. Unfortunately, too many rocks and boulders inhibit the depth. One side of the fall is partially scarred by fire, but there's some mature beach and hickory with excellent shade. It's worth the short trip. On the way you pass some pretty good rock faces, 25 and 30 feet tall. They contain the namesake cave, really only a rock fissure about 15 feet deep and five feet wide.

The water is a little bit murky from sediment likely caused by erosion that followed the 2000 wildfire. Much of the hike is through the burn area. Great wildflowers as a result.

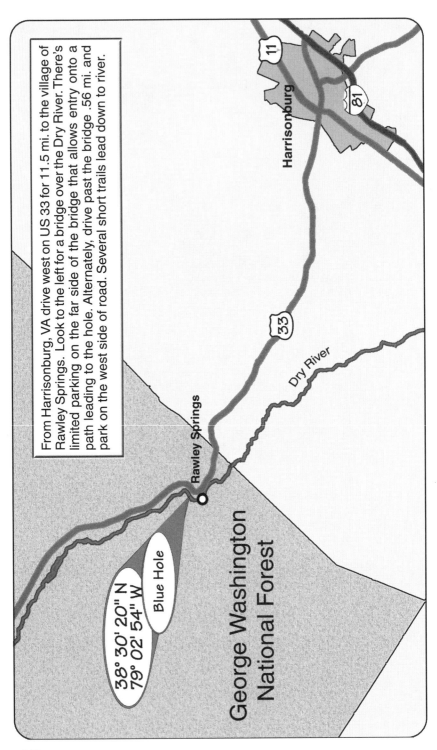

From Harrisonburg, VA drive west on US 33 for 11.5 mi. to the village of Rawley Springs. Look to the left for a bridge over the Dry River. There's limited parking on the far side of the bridge that allows entry onto a path leading to the hole. Alternately, drive past the bridge .56 mi. and park on the west side of road. Several short trails lead down to river.

Harrisonburg

Dry River

Rawley Springs

38° 30' 20" N
79° 02' 54" W

Blue Hole

George Washington
National Forest

Dry River

A spring under the principal diving rock keeps the hole filled with water, even during drought. Buck Rexrode, a lifelong resident of Rockingham County said that until a flood in 1985 there was a tunnel you could swim through. Rexrode, a former state boxing champ in the 133-pound class, was considerably more hydrodynamic than his current outline, pictured above.

"The flood tilted the rock back five or ten degrees to where a good ol' boy like me can't get through there no more."

Rexrode has been a regular at Blue Hole even since before he was born. His father was from Franklin, WV and his mother was from Harrisonburg, VA. Blue Hole was approximately midway and that's where the young couple got together one summer day in 1958.

"My mother always told me the reason I was so small was that half of me floated down the Dry River during conception."

Rexrode still honors the place by spending afternoons fishing with his son and picking up the bales of garbage that roadside swimming holes like this collect. He also composed and posted this friendly reminder:

Ain't this a great place to swim.
We hope that you come back again.
When you read this please don't pout,
What you carry in please carry it back out.

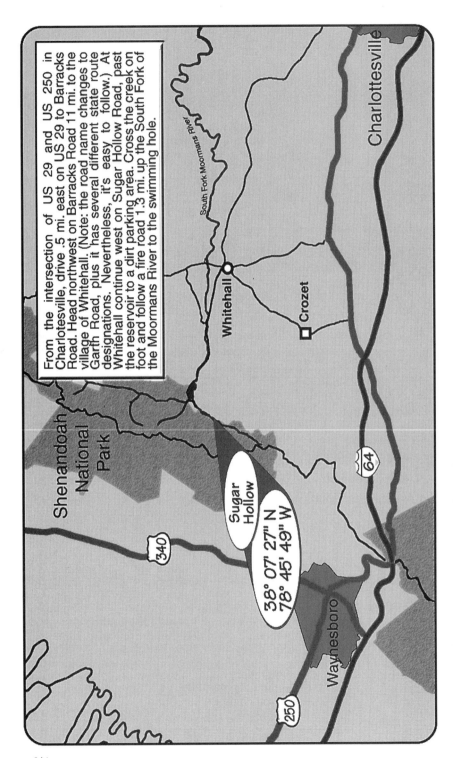

Sugar Hollow

Charlottesville's swimming hole. It's about and formed by some rock that's tilted at a low angle across the stream at the top of the hole. The rock ends the water flares into a pool about 20 feet in diameter. The cascade has burrowed out a good sweet spot as much as ten feet deep. I was able to dive off the rock to the left of the fall on the trail side of the hole. Nothing like a jump though. Just a shallow dive.

The biggest liability is lack of seating. There's only room for about a half dozen people to perch comfortably, and there's apt to be many more visitors than that on a weekend. Water is very turbid with visibility no more than two feet. That might simply have been due to a recent rain. The South Fork of the Moorman River is within the Shenandoah National Park, hence it's a well-protected watershed.

In sum, a good swimming hole. If it were a car it would be a two–door sedan, which is to say nothing fancy. Worth a visit when Charlottesville gets too hot.

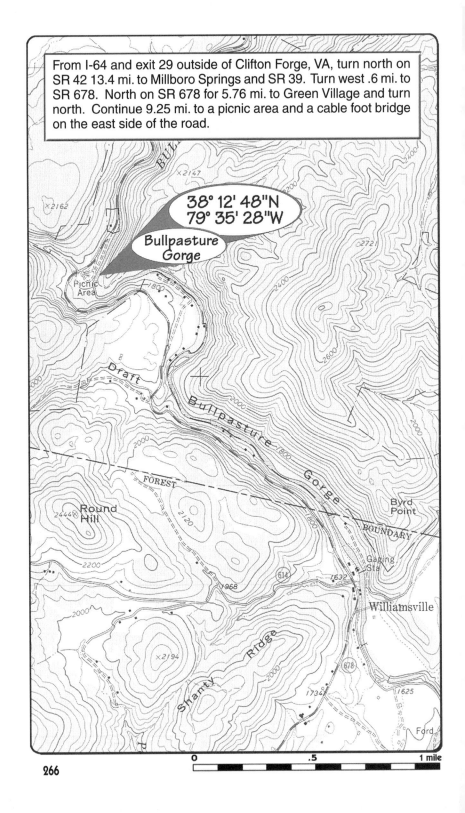

From I-64 and exit 29 outside of Clifton Forge, VA, turn north on SR 42 13.4 mi. to Millboro Springs and SR 39. Turn west .6 mi. to SR 678. North on SR 678 for 5.76 mi. to Green Village and turn north. Continue 9.25 mi. to a picnic area and a cable foot bridge on the east side of the road.

38° 12' 48"N
79° 35' 28"W

Bullpasture Gorge

Picnic Area

Draft

Bullpasture Gorge

FOREST

Round Hill

×2444

Byrd Point

BOUNDARY

Gaging Sta

614

1632

Williamsville

2200

1968

×2194

Shanty Ridge

678

1734

1625

Ford

0   .5   1 mile

Bullpasture Gorge

A cable bridge stretches from the parking area across Bullpasture Gorge to a sand and gravel beach. There is a low wall on the west at an outside bend in the river and as you might expect, a beach on the inside turn. It's mainly gravel with mixed hardwoods. One of the trees provides a rope swing. It's about 10 feet high. Get good clearance on the swing, 'cause without any impound downstream, the depth is not that great. If you are skeptical about the safety of the swing, there are a couple of low rock launches on the west that stand over deeper water.

The pool is quite open, 70 feet long and 20 feet wide with a riffle below. Hard to think of it as a "gorge," though. Users have piled rocks downstream to improve the impound. It raises the water level by as much as 18 inches, turning what would be an insignificant spot into a marginally good swimming hole. Just around the corner is another swimming spot with similar dimensions. Easy access. Lots of sun. Lots of kids.

It's in the Highland Wildlife Management Area. There is some agriculture upstream, but it doesn't seem to be very intensive. Not like some huge pig barn or a poultry operation that produces tons of waste per week.

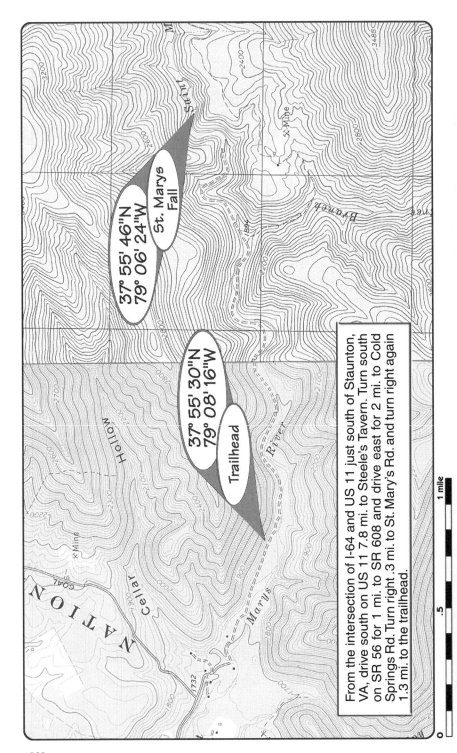

37° 55' 46"N
79° 06' 24"W

St. Marys
Fall

37° 55' 30"N
79° 08' 16"W

Trailhead

From the intersection of I-64 and US 11 just south of Staunton, VA, drive south on US 11 7.8 mi. to Steele's Tavern. Turn south on SR 56 for 1 mi. to SR 608 and drive east for 2 mi. to Cold Springs Rd. Turn right .3 mi. to St. Mary's Rd. and turn right again 1.3 mi. to the trailhead.

0   .5   1 mile

St. Mary's River

A hiker approaches the fall along a bench of land backed by a crag thirty feet high. Twelve feet above the creek and directly opposite the fall, the ledge ends abruptly, leaving you — a hot, sweaty observer — staring down at a tank of water 10 feet deep. What do you do? That's a rhetorical question, of course. You jump.

The pool is around twenty feet long and oriented at 90 degrees to the fall face. It's aesthetically pleasing since the sides are generally solid stone and arranged at straight angles, giving it a rectangular form. Plus the water is exquisite. Cool, clean runoff from the top of the St. Mary's Wilderness. The deepest water is under the ledge, where it appears that about 25 cubic feet of rock simply disappeared. The pool faces west, so it ought to be good in the afternoon, even though the canopy partially covers the creek. There's about 150 square feet of seating, which is unlikely to accommodate the number of people you'll find here on a weekend.

The St. Mary's Fall Trail begins in the George Washington National Forest on the north bank of the river. You might see one or two blue blazes on the way to the first crossing at 1.1 miles. From the ford continue .2 miles to the junction with St. Mary's Trail and continue upstream a short distance, then cross back to the north bank. It's .6 miles and one more ford to reach the fall.

Smoke Hole

38° 50' 32"N
79° 17' 06"W

Lots of people talk about Smoke Hole as a swimming spot. Not my opinion. South Branch of the Potomac River doesn't have any great rock structure.

Panther Falls

37° 43' 07"N
79° 17' 24"W

It almost achieves water park status. A couple of very good falls, the highest is around nine feet. Good jumps. Lots of people.

Shoe Creek

37° 47' 50"N
79° 05' 54"W

Probably worth a visit. There's a cascade on the creek and a basin with a zip line running across it. Good thing it's a zip line, 'cause the water isn't deep enough for jumping and there's nothing to jump from anyway.

Statons Falls

37° 46' 07"N
79° 14' 13"W

Tall fall right on a secondary state road. Very pretty, but only marginal as a swimming spot.

Goshen Pass

37° 55' 11"N
79° 26' 02"W

People always talk about driving up Goshen Pass to swim in the Maury River. Maybe the water was to low when I reviewed it, but it looked like a boulder-strewn riverbed. No really good impound to create a hole.

Alone Mill

37° 51' 00"N
79° 25' 20"W

Maury River. The bridge on County Route 622 and a minor rock face, maybe a 10 foot climb. Large gravel beach and lots of the usual litter including car parts.

Campbell Creek

37° 52' 14"N
79° 00' 22"W

Take State Route 56 to the access for the Appalachian Trail. Climb to the Mau-Har trail and the hole is where the trail veers right and starts a climb up the stream. Not worth the trip unless you're on the trail anyway.

Richardson Gorge

38° 01' 49"N
79° 53' 41"W

Nothing deep or interesting.

Index

Swimming Holes of California features 105 hikes. Swimming season in California lasts about 140 days, starting April 15 in the southern deserts and ending early October in the Sierra, Using those numbers, calculations show that only once in more than 2,000 years will it not be perfect at a swimming hole somewhere in California.

Have fun checking the math.

256 Pages
137 Photos
70 Maps
ISBN 0-9657686-4-3

A backcountry tip sheet that surveys more than 200 creeks and canyons from the high plateaus of Utah to the Mexican border. Splash Southwest features plunge pools that're scuba deep, tall river canyons with long pools for lap swimming and perennial creeks where the sand is thick and the shade is dense.

Day Trips with a Splash

Swimming Holes of the Southwest

218 Pages
230 Photos
51 Maps
ISBN 0-96576862-7

From the blue springs of Florida through north Georgia and the Smoky Mountains, Southeastern Swimming Holes extends to the southern Appalachians to include Eastern Tennessee, Kentucky and the Cumberland Plateau.

DAY TRIPS WITH A SPLASH:

SWIMMING HOLES OF THE SOUTHEAST

Due Spring 2003